THE MAGICAL THOUGHTS OF GRIEVING CHILDREN

TREATING CHILDREN WITH COMPLICATED MOURNING AND ADVICE FOR PARENTS

James A. Fogarty, ED.D.

Licensed Clinical Psychologist
Certified School Psychologist

Death, Value and Meaning Series
Series Editor: John D. Morgan

Baywood Publishing Company, Inc.
AMITYVILLE, NEW YORK

Library of Congress Catalog Number: 99-046201
ISBN: 0-89503-205-8 (Cloth)
ISBN: 0-89503-206-6 (Paper)

Library of Congress Cataloging-in-Publication Data

Fogarty, James A., 1953–
    The magical thoughts of grieving children : treating children with complicated
mourning and advice for parents / James A. Fogarty.
        p. cm. - - (Death, value, and meaning series)
    Includes bibliographical references and index.
    ISBN 0-89503-205-8 (cloth : alk. paper) - - ISBN 0-89503-206-6 (paper : alk. paper)
        1. Grief in children. 2. Magical thinking in children. I. Title. II. Series.

BF723.G75 F64 1999
155.9'37'083- -dc21

                                                                        99-046201

Dedication

Ninety percent of success is picking the right partners in life. I dedicate this book to two great partners: God and my wife, Cyndy. I also dedicate this book to two extraordinary boys who are on the verge of becoming men, my sons Jason and Shawn.

Acknowledgments

After twenty years of counseling families with grief, it is impossible to adequately thank them for allowing me to learn from their most intimate moments and to experience their progress as they healed after the death of their loved ones. Simple expressions are often the best—thank you.

When writing a book it is helpful to have a caring family, which I have been blessed with. I would like to acknowledge my wife, Cyndy, for giving me an incredible opportunity to write. I would also like to offer my appreciation for my children, Jason and Shawn, who would always check-in with me to see how my books are developing, often with encouragement and affectionate commentary.

Writing a book is a tremendous effort and on occasion as I was writing, my brain would stop functioning. When this happened, I reached for the telephone and I called someone who would ignite my brain with ideas, Judy Carra-Engblom, a leader in Hospice.

I appreciate the assistance that Joanne Wolfgram offered in reviewing my books and offered me all of the lessons I ignored when I was in high school English class.

I especially appreciate the efforts of Dr. John Morgan of King's College and Stuart Cohen and the staff of Baywood Publishing.

As always, thank you God.

Contents

Introduction   1

CHAPTER 1
Children's View of Grief   5

CHAPTER 2
Cognition: The Most Definitive Feature of Children's Grief . .   25

CHAPTER 3
The Model of Magical Thought   49

CHAPTER 4
The Tasks of Healthy Mourning Distorted by Destructive
Magical Thought   65

CHAPTER 5
Action-Focused Techniques to Eliminate Destructive
Magical Thought 103

CHAPTER 6
Anger and Magical Thought 137

CHAPTER 7
A Special Note for Parents 153

CHAPTER 8
Magical Thoughts of Adults and Our Society 165

CHAPTER 9
Final Thoughts 173

APPENDIX A
Resources for Action-Focused Techniques 175

References 177

Index 179

Introduction

Truth and Reality:
The Cures for Destructive Magical Thought

Magical thought is children's inaccurate conclusion(s) regarding a loss experience resulting in children believing that they are responsible for the loss experience and need to fix the loss experience. Magical thought may lead children to believe that they have developed a method of mourning, but they have actually developed an unhealthy and complicated process of mourning.

Dr. James A. Fogarty

There have been many excellent theorists, researchers, and practitioners who have offered insights and knowledge about grief. Elisabeth Kübler-Ross (1969) laid the foundation to understanding mourning as a separate entity that theorists and researchers have been able to utilize in the development of grief theories, models, research, and treatment strategies. As examples, Elisabeth Kübler-Ross (1969, 1983) offered her insights about grief emotions. William Worden (1982) has contributed a model regarding the tasks of mourning that helps grief therapists understand the form and structure of normal grief. In the area of dysfunctional grief, Kenneth Doka (1989) has studied disenfranchised grief, Therese Rando (1993) continues to offer significant research on the many issues of complicated mourning, and others have offered ideas and studies regarding various types of complicated mourning. Contributing to the understanding of children's thought processes is Jean Piaget (1979), who has provided a foundation to conceptualize the development of childhood cognition, which grief therapists can apply to children who are experiencing grief.

Having all of this valuable knowledge available, what I have often wondered is, "How do I determine my exact clinical point of treatment when I am trying to assist a child who is engaged in a process of complicated mourning?" In other words, how do I know which of many complicated mourning issues I should address when I have a child sitting in front of me needing my help? How can I determine which of the many complicated issues a child is experiencing needs to be processed right now? For example, many years ago I counseled a sixteen-year-old female who had experienced the deaths of eleven people in her short lifetime. Four of the deaths were suicides and two of the suicides were her family members. With all of the many dimensions of complication that these many losses create, where do I begin with assisting this child?

These questions are why I developed the "Model of Magical Thought"—to help with the treatment of children who are experiencing a dysfunctional and complicated process of grief and mourning. It is my hope that when the reader finishes this book, the reader will have a structure that incorporates the work of researchers combined with the Model of Magical Thought. The Model of Magical Thought offers a very practical and workable method of treatment for grief therapists, caregivers, and parents who assist children with complicated mourning. This book is designed for the variety of professionals who assist children experiencing complicated mourning and it is also designed for parents who want to better understand their children's grief reactions and want to work more effectively with their children's grief therapists. Although I am not suggesting that parents offer grief therapy (the treatment of complicated mourning) to their own children, I fully understand the incredible importance of parents. I realize that parental awareness about children's grief allows parents to make better decisions regarding the treatment and competency of their children's grief therapist.

The first two chapters of this book lay the foundation for the Model of Magical Thought, by offering the normal and healthy grief emotions that are expected when children have experienced the death of a loved one. The purpose of each normal grief emotion is also discussed. One of the most significant factors that defines children's grief as different from adult grief is thoroughly discussed in this book—children's cognitive development. The discussion of children's cognition offers a comprehensive description of children's cognitive development useful to clinicians, noting that children's cognitive equipment is incomplete, which leaves children susceptible to destructive magical thought related to their process of mourning. The third chapter of this book offers the Model of Magical Thought. Children's magical thought is defined and the effects of destructive magical thought are described. Included in this chapter is a discussion on the concept that grief and destructive magical thought develop as children's personality develops. A structure will be offered that demonstrates how magical thought is so powerful, that for some children (not all) it could influence the development of personality disorders as they mature. In the fourth chapter, the tasks of healthy mourning will be detailed as well as the many ways children's mourning can become complicated. The many parts of the first four chapters will converge to form a guide for the reader to identify healthy grief, diagnose complicated mourning, and determine the current clinical point of treatment. The fifth chapter discusses action-focused techniques offering treatment methods utilized with the Model of Magical Thought, while also considering the cognitive development of children. The treatment portion of this book will focus on the utilization of action-focused techniques to eliminate destructive magical thought and assist children and families to process healthy mourning. There will also be specialized chapters within this book focusing on children's grief-related anger coupled with magical thought, cultural magical thought, and a special chapter for parents with children who are actively experiencing grief resulting from the death of a loved one.

A SPECIAL NOTE TO THE READER
PROFESSIONALS AND PARENTS

For those of you who have chosen to make a career of giving care to bereaved children, many blessings will naturally come to you. One of the many blessings you will receive is that you will learn more about yourself than you would as a member of any other professional group. Learning about you is not self-centered, as it is a natural part of helping grief-stricken children. The more you know about yourself, the more you will be able to help others because you have gifts to offer that those who never consider death and never help children, will never acquire. Your gifts to children will help calm anger, lessen anguish, reduce pining, enhance bonding, develop spirituality, and teach reality. Many of the best personal and professional insights I have ever received were from bereaved children who offered their own gifts freely to others. Gifts of honestly saying what is on their mind. Gifts of questioning the fear that adults have with the topic of death. Gifts of expressing reality when adults have ignored it. Gifts of telling caregivers what they need to have in their office to help children who are attempting to mourn. Gifts of reminding adults what it is like to think and feel like a child. Gifts of making adults experience a deep feeling of humbleness. Gifts of resilience reflected in children's incredible ability to bounce back. Gifts in telling us what they feel through their behavior. Gifts, gifts, and more gifts all freely offered to us, assuming our ears and eyes are open. Caregivers, professionals, and volunteers who assist bereaved children must have their ears and eyes wide open when they are with children who are mourning.

For those readers who are parents of bereaved children, you are learning more about yourself and grief than you probably ever wanted. The fact that you are motivated to learn more about your children's grief enhances the probability that your children will progress with healthy mourning. There is truth in the notion that children absorb the functional and dysfunctional elements of their parents. Although you may have been motivated to read this book to help your children, I have a suggestion. Read this book twice. The first time you read this book, read it to discover how grief affected you as a child, teenager, and adult. The more you understand your own process of mourning, the better you can help your children. Without knowledge about our own losses and the associated process of mourning, we are handicapped in our effectiveness to help others. Read this book a second time considering your children's grief and the behavioral reactions you are observing from your children. After reading this book, you will have a finely tuned ear for children's destructive magical thought, which will help assist you in determining if your children are experiencing healthy versus a complicated process of mourning. There is a special section in this book for parents which offers "red flags" that help parents determine if it is time to get professional treatment for their children as well as criteria to determine if a therapist is really competent in the treatment of grief issues and complicated mourning. The treatment methods described in this book are for therapists and it is not recommended that parents act as grief therapists. However, parents are the front-line of support for children and the parental role is always the most vital in offering support and stability. It is helpful for parents to know what to typically expect from bereaved children and from a grief therapist who counsels children with complicated mourning. This book will offer you information about children's normal grief reactions, as well as offer an understanding of what grief therapists are trying to accomplish when offering therapy to children who have developed complications with their process of mourning. By understanding the latter, parents and grief therapists can work more efficiently together to assist children.

CHAPTER 1

Children's View of Grief

The focus of this and the next chapter is to lay a foundation before presenting the Model of Magical Thought. This chapter will offer a brief idea of how children come to realize which adults in their lives are experts about grief. This chapter offers a more extensive discussion of the normal and expected emotions of children's grief and each grief emotion's purpose.

HOW TO BE AN EXPERT IN THE
EYES OF CHILDREN

Children may not understand the difference between a psychologist, social worker, nurse, or hospice volunteer as these words are too abstract for their comprehension. How do bereaved children determine if the adults assisting them are experts? Often, bereaved children ask helping adults what losses they have experienced. Their questioning helps children determine for themselves if the helping adults are truly experts in the process of mourning. Is it appropriate for professionals and caregivers assisting bereaved children to talk about their own grief experiences and reactions? Each adult would have to answer this question individually. This author advocates that it is valuable to discuss our own losses with children, but this author offers a qualifier. This author believes that it is appropriate for adults to share personal losses with children only if those losses have been well processed. Although training is very important and quite necessary because grief is a very specialized issue, a well processed loss coupled with excellent training in the treatment of grief and complicated mourning are very effective tools for grief therapists and other caregivers who assist bereaved children. This book offers an opportunity for you to not only consider the losses of children you are assisting, but also your own. Well processed grief and a thorough process of mourning offer lessons and gifts that caring adults can offer to children who are mourning the death of a loved one.

A NEW LOOK AT THE NORMAL EMOTIONS OF CHILDREN'S GRIEF

What are the healthy and normal grief emotions that children are expected to experience when a close loved one has died? What are the purposes of each of the healthy and normal grief emotions that children experience?

Emotions are like everything else that exists in this world; they have a purpose and a reason for being. One purpose of emotions is that they offer messages as well as lessons for children to learn. Another purpose of emotions is that emotional expressions from one person elicit emotional reactions in other people, which create bonds. This is especially true for the normal grief emotions. *This author defines normal grief emotions as the emotions that share the common purpose of helping children to continue on a process of healthy mourning.* Most children do not realize that grief emotions are normal and have a healthy purpose. With incomplete cognitive equipment, children often interpret their normal grief emotions inaccurately, resulting in the application of destructive magical thought, which disrupts the normal process of mourning, creating greater opportunity for the development of complicated mourning.

THE NORMAL GRIEF EMOTIONS

The Numb and Stunned Reaction

When I was a child I had a very favorite uncle. This uncle loved horses and he loved children, which made for wonderful weekends on his ranch for many years. Every weekend we would gather at his ranch and joyfully work with him and his horses. He had such an incredible Old Irish personality that he could make cleaning a barn hysterically fun. When I was fourteen years of age, this wonderful old man was unexpectedly killed in a car accident. On a foggy night he apparently thought he was driving over a bridge when he was actually on the side of a bridge in an extended parking area. His car went into the rain-swollen Rock River and he was killed. My very large Irish Catholic family gathered together at my grandmother's home after we heard of his death. Within this large family gathering was every emotional grief reaction imaginable. Since I was very close to this uncle I thought it was peculiar that I felt no emotional reaction.

Many bereaved children today also have experienced this strange phenomenon that grief therapists know as a numb and stunned reaction. Often children describe their numb and stunned reaction as not being able to remember their dead loved ones' facial features, the sound of their voice, or the memories of activities they did together. Numb and stunned is a normal and common grief reaction, which offers a defensive and protective barrier, designed to allow children to gradually incorporate their normal grief emotions. Bereaved children do not realize that their numb and stunned reactions are normal and common. Children may only realize that every family member around them is offering a variety of emotional reactions to the death of the loved one, which they do not feel. It is natural for children to try to incorporate their numb and stunned reactions into their thinking by attempting to interpret these reactions. Often, children's interpretations of normal numb and stunned reactions are self-deprecatory. When asked about their numb and stunned reactions, children will often respond, "I thought something was wrong with me" or "I thought I didn't care enough." It is important to note that children experiencing normal grief reactions, such as numb and stunned, also have incomplete cognitive equipment, which advances interpretations that are inaccurate and often self-deprecatory, leading to the potential development of destructive magical thought.

The Purposes of Numb and Stunned

The purposes of bereaved children's initial numb and stunned reactions are several. Numb and stunned reactions protect bereaved children from being overwhelmed by all of their intense grief emotions related to the loss experience by offering children a gradual incorporation of the loss. Numb and stunned reactions also signal children that something unusual and significant has happened, and that they will need to make adjustments. Typically, children's emotions are readily accessible to children. The inaccessibility of emotions suggests to children that something unusual has occurred. Numb and stunned reactions are a way children "brace" themselves emotionally following a trauma. It is like the feel of a taunt seatbelt just before a car accident suggesting, "Brace yourself." Numb and stunned reactions allow children to gather information objectively and observe others. The numb and stunned reaction also allows children to wait until they feel safe before experiencing the more intense emotions of grief and proceeding through a process of mourning.

Although it is difficult for adults to bond with children who are experiencing a numb and stunned reaction, this reaction can enter the mix of family dynamics. For example, a parent who does not have much knowledge about children's grief reactions may observe a calm and relaxed child shortly after the death of a significant loved one in a different light than a parent who understands the child's grief. A parent, with knowledge about grief reactions, may conclude that the child is not mourning intensively right now and this parent may appreciate the lack of emotional response from the child, realizing grief reactions may come later. Another parent, without knowledge of grief reactions, may negatively interpret this child's behavior as obviously not caring much for the dead family member, and send signals to the child that the child is not mourning correctly. Criticisms for not mourning correctly may be supported by parental and family reactions to the child's lack of emotional response or may also develop within the child's thinking without parental assistance. This negative interpretation often results in the bereaved child defining a normal grief reaction as abnormal, creating an emotional paradox:

> I need to demonstrate grief emotions like everyone else, even though I do not feel any grief emotions.

A mourning child in this paradox may fake emotional reactions, diverting the child from the actual tasks of healthy mourning, which include feeling grief reactions such as numb and stunned. This may result in the bereaved child concluding:

> I cannot feel anything about my dead loved one, so I am abnormal.

Bereaved children with this aversive conclusion may start to believe that normal grief emotions (numb and stunned) are abnormal, or they may conclude that they are abnormal. Often children with this aberrant conclusion may attach magical thought, which leads bereaved children away from normal grief reactions, and stops them from progressing through a healthy process of mourning. Consider another possible conclusion bereaved children may have regarding their numb and stunned reactions:

> I don't feel anything, so I obviously did not care enough.

This is a self-judgment that, if it becomes persistent, has the potential to devastate children's entire personality development.

Children's negative thoughts/conclusions may eventually develop into magical thought creating long-term difficulties and complicated mourning.

Offering children a simple explanation about the normalcy of numb and stunned reactions and their purposes often reduces or eliminates the aversive effects of children's misinterpretation of their numb and stunned reactions. Numb and stunned reactions need to be explained to children in specific concrete terms.

PARENT SUGGESTION

Parents can offer their children this explanation about numb and stunned reactions:

If you do not feel anything right now, it is okay. Right after someone dies, many children do not feel any emotions for a period of time. That's normal. It will go away in a while. If it does not go away, make sure you tell us. When it goes away you will have other feelings that do not feel normal, but they usually are. Make sure you tell us about those feelings too.

This explanation allows children to realize that all their grief emotions will come, which is a healthy expectation that may help children feel more normal when other grief emotions occur. Without explanation of numb and stunned reactions, bereaved children have an untrained and bountiful imagination that could create a variety of potentially destructive magical thoughts, that they could attach to their process of mourning creating complicated mourning.

Commotion

Commotion is behavior exhibited by bereaved children based on the combination of the excessive energy, attentional difficulties, tension, and fear that children display when experiencing grief reactions. The word commotion is an appropriate descriptor because many children demonstrate this reaction through very active behavior. Bereaved children exhibiting commotion often appear to resemble children with Attention Deficit Hyperactivity Disorder (ADHD). The following list is a review of the symptoms of ADHD from the *Diagnostic and Statistical Manual of Mental Disorders, Fourth Edition*. Copyright 1994 American Psychiatric Association. Reprinted with permission.

A. Either (1) or (2)

(1) six (or more) of the following symptoms of inattention for at least six months to a degree that is maladaptive and inconsistent with developmental level:

Inattention

  (a) often fails to give close attention to details or makes careless mistakes in schoolwork, work, or other activities
  (b) often has difficulty sustaining attention in tasks or play activities
  (c) often does not seem to listen when spoken to directly
  (d) often does not follow through on instructions and fails to finish schoolwork, chores, or duties in the workplace (not due to oppositional behavior or failure to understand instructions)
  (e) often has difficulty organizing tasks and activities
  (f) often avoids, dislikes, or is reluctant to engage in tasks that require sustained mental effort
  (g) often loses things necessary for tasks or activities
  (h) is often easily distracted by extraneous stimuli
  (i) is often forgetful in daily activities.

(2) six or more of the following symptoms of hyperactivity-impulsivity have persisted for at least six months to a degree that is maladaptive and inconsistent with developmental level:

Hyperactivity

  (a) often fidgets with hands and feet and squirms in seat
  (b) often leaves seat in classroom or in other situations in which remaining seated is expected
  (c) often runs or climbs excessively in situations in which it is inappropriate
  (d) often has difficulty playing or engaging in leisure activities quietly
  (e) is often "on the go" or acts as if "driven by a motor"
  (f) often talks excessively.

Impulsivity

  (g) often blurts out answers before questions have been completed
  (h) often has difficulty waiting turn
  (i) often interrupts or intrudes on others.

B. Some hyperactive-impulsive or inattentive symptoms that caused impairment were present before age seven years.

C. Some impairment from the symptoms is present in two or more settings (e.g., school and home).

D. There must be clear evidence of clinically significant impairment in social, academic, or occupational functioning.

Commotion resembles ADHD because it has many of the symptoms that are reflected in the above diagnostic criteria for ADHD. ADHD has been well researched and it does exist, but how much of what is diagnosed as ADHD is really ADHD? Is the grief reaction of commotion ever misdiagnosed as ADHD? ADHD does have a history of being misdiagnosed. Paul de Mesquite and Walter Gilliam (1994) indicate that there is an overlap of symptoms with ADHD and uncomplicated bereavement. Jean Thomas (1996) suggests that there is a tendency to mislabel Post-Traumatic Stress Disorder or Traumatic Stress Disorder as ADHD. PTSD is often associated with complicated mourning (e.g., witnessing a violent death). Weller, Weller, and Fristad (1995) have found that bipolar disorder and ADHD are often confused. Nils Lies (1992) states that ADHD is often the misdiagnosis for conduct disorder and antisocial problems. The potential for misdiagnosing ADHD is great.

ADHD OR COMMOTION?

Consider the case of ten-year-old Tommy as an example of a bereaved child misdiagnosed with ADHD. He had been previously diagnosed as having ADHD and medications for ADHD were administered with an unsuccessful result. It was eventually decided that all of the appropriate assessments would be administered to Tommy to determine the existence of ADHD. Every cognitive, neuro-psychological, and achievement assessment device administered to Tommy offered a normal result. The existence of ADHD for Tommy was not apparent in spite of his many ADHD-like mannerisms.

A developmental history was taken to determine other possible factors that may have been creating Tommy's excessive behavior. It was found that when Tommy was six months old, his brother died of cancer. His mother and father had to make many medical decisions to extend their ill child's life. Disagreements on the medical deci-sions ensued. When Tommy's brother died his parents reviewed their medical decisions and disagreements, which included a strong element of projected blame. Within their relationship, the defense mechanism of projection of blame grew between them. For three years they had a very dysfunctional, hostile, and complicated mourning process within their family. From the time that Tommy was six months of age until he was three and one half years of age he was experiencing and absorbing his parents' intense, hostile, and very dysfunctional process of complicated mourning. After three years of experiencing this complicated mourning process, Tommy's parents agreed to marital therapy and they successfully worked through their issues. Their marital relationship stabilized and calmed, but Tommy did not. Tommy had been absorbing an extremely hostile and dysfunctional process of complicated mourning at a time when his immature cognitive development could offer no psychological defense mechanisms. His grief-related commotion was in high gear and commotion became a strong component of his developing personality.

Often children are diagnosed with ADHD and medicated by a physician who may only review the symptoms that are described by parents or other adults who have knowledge of the overactive children. To offer medicines without adequate assessments is a frightening method of treatment. Commotion, which is very active behavior founded on feelings of frailty, tension, fear, and associated excessive energy, resembles ADHD. It is important that mental health professionals take a comprehensive history of children's development, including all loss experiences, which will aid in the determination of the existence of commotion reactions associated with grief. Administering appropriate cognitive and neuro-psychological evaluations to children will also assist in ruling out or confirming the diagnosis of ADHD.

PARENT SUGGESTION

Parents should accept a diagnosis of ADHD for their children only after appropriate assessments have been completed which would include a cognitive assessment, neuro-psychological assessment, achievement assessment, and a complete history of their children's development, especially loss experiences.

The Purposes of Commotion

Commotion calls attention to others that children are mourning. Due to a lack of complete cognitive equipment, children cannot often verbalize their grief fears, tensions, worries, and heightened feelings of frailty. Commotion allows children to express grief issues through their behavior with the goal of gaining the attention and assistance of adults, which children may not be able to express verbally. Commotion allows bereaved children a simple element of empowerment. Through commotion, children feel a sense of empowerment in all of their environments such as school, home, and daycare. By exhibiting commotion, bereaved children's increased activity level offers them the "center place" in their environments, as all environments may eventually develop around their grief-related commotion. For example, a bereaved child may actually stop a classroom from functioning with excessive behavior due to grief-related commotion, thus giving the child a feeling of empowerment the child needs.

Since commotion is calling attention to children's grief, commotion can be utilized as a wonderful barometer that helps adults realize that children need to express some aspect of grief. Commotion allows supportive adults the opportunity to set up conditions that give bereaved children the potential to express their grief.

Attempts to Re-Create Coupled with Balancing Denial

After the death of a loved one children have a strong desire to get their dead loved one back. They attempt to re-create the situations and experiences they had available when their dead loved one was alive. Children's attempts to re-create those lost experiences (founded on longing, searching, and pining) are a normal grief reaction designed to fail.

When I was fourteen years of age and my favorite uncle (who owned the horse ranch) had been dead for two months, I had another very nice uncle who offered to take me to the ranch to work with the horses. I was excited to go to attempt to re-create those lost experiences, but I readily realized that it just was not the same. Although this was a very kind uncle and special in his own way, the unique features of the original uncle were not there.

Children's "attempts to re-create" are designed to fail, as they should. Consider Sigmund Freud's 1929 comment on this topic quoted by Therese Rando (1993):

> Although we know that after such a loss the acute state of mourning will subside, we also know that we shall remain inconsolable and will never find a substitute. No matter what may fill the gap, even if it is filled completely, it nevertheless remains something else. And actually, this is how it should be. It is the only way of perpetuating that love which we do not have to relinquish (p. 81).

Children who attempt to re-create what they had when the dead loved one was alive are screaming, "I want my loved one back."

Freud describes quite well children's desire to re-create what they lost, but what do their "attempts to re-create" have to do with denial? Consider Therese Rando's (1993) statements about a definition of denial:

> (Two) forms of denial can be found in complicated mourning. Denial of the fact of the death is more pathological and difficult to sustain; denial of the impact, significance, and implications of the death is often obscured under the external knowledge that the death did occur in reality (p. 115).

When reality is not accepted there is a greater potential for the development of distorted conclusions regarding the death of a loved one. Many children search to re-create what they had when the dead loved one was alive. They may try to "people replace"—by forcing others to be exactly like the dead person. Children may also revisit those special places where they had been with their dead loved one to attempt to re-create moments when they were together. When children attempt to re-create but cannot attain exactly what they had with their dead loved one, their "attempts to re-create" help children realize their loved one is dead. Children's "attempts to re-create" what they had but cannot attain balance denial by demonstrating the reality that the dead loved one *is* actually dead. "Attempts to re-create" remind children:

> *You can't have your dead loved one back.*

When children are firmly entrenched in denial about the death of a loved one, it is very likely these children are either stopping themselves and/or are being stopped by others from their "attempts to re-create." For example, a boy's father dies. His father had a favorite chair in the living room that he always sat in when he was alive; it was called "Dad's chair." After his father's death, this boy walked into the living room and without looking toward his father's chair, he started to talk to his father. He eventually looked toward the chair and realized that his father was not in his chair. Then he remembered that his father was not there because his father is dead. This boy's desire and "attempt to re-create" reminded him of the reality that his father is dead, reducing his denial. What if his mother, with good intentions, went into the living room after his father's death and eliminated all of the old furniture and replaced it and then painted the entire room a different color? All of the visual cues are now gone, including Dad's chair. Without these cues this boy would walk into the living room and may never start to talk to his father. By changing the room, his mother eliminated the visual cues that would activate this boy's "attempts to re-create," resulting in him not experiencing this reminder of his father's death, and enhancing denial rather than reducing it.

PARENT SUGGESTION

A common question many parents will ask grief therapists is if it is a good idea not to go back to their favorite vacation spot now that a loved one is dead. Unless there is a special circumstance, families should be advised to go back to their favorite vacation spot because it is an opportunity for children to attempt to re-create, which will assist children in minimizing denial.

The Purposes of Children's "Attempts to Re-Create"

The obvious purpose of children's "attempts to re-create" is that "attempts to re-create" help children realize the reality that their loved one is dead, because "attempts to re-create" are designed to fail. Children's natural attempts to re-create their relationship with their dead loved one helps keep denial to a healthy minimum. "Attempts to re-create" also help children to accept a very hard reality on a daily basis with small, but very significant events, reminding children that their loved one is dead. Children's failures to re-create their cherished experiences with their dead loved ones offers children the reality; "You cannot have the dead person back." "Attempts to re-create" also allow children to realize the importance of the dead person. It is quite an irony that a person is not fully appreciated until after the person has died. "Attempts to re-create" assist children in developing a full appreciation and understanding of the dead loved one's impact on their life. Children need to attempt to re-create and they need an explanation that their attempts to re-create are normal, but they will never be able to regain the unique qualities of their dead loved one.

Anguish

Anguish is a very abstract and difficult word for children to understand. A very concrete way of expressing anguish so it is understandable to concrete thinking children is to describe anguish as, "that empty feeling you have deep inside ever since the death of your loved one." Anguish is the most difficult of the grief emotions for parents to allow their children to experience. Quality and caring parents with good intentions will often stop their children from experiencing the normal grief emotion of anguish.

I was counseling an anguished eight-year-old boy whose brother had previously died. His parents were concerned with his degree of isolation in his bedroom. He was not having any positive interaction with family and friends as he spent all of his time isolated in his bedroom. Because he spent so much time in his bedroom, I happened to ask him a question that I now ask every bereaved child I counsel. I asked him, "What do you have in your bedroom?" He took a deep breath and replied, "A television with a built in VCR, remote control and I have cable with HBO and Cinemax. I have eight remote control cars and one remote control helicopter. I have a private line because I am on the Internet and I have a computer. I have another private line because I have a telephone answering machine and here is my beeper. I have a heated waterbed. I have three guitars. I have fish—200 fish." He continued for ten minutes listing all of the many items in his bedroom.

When this eight-year-old boy felt the grief emotion of anguish, he got a new toy from his parents. What might this boy conclude about the process of mourning, himself, and/or his parents? Common conclusions formulated from children in this situation include:

I need to stop feeling anguish.

I should handle grief by distracting myself.

My parents think something is wrong with me when I feel anguish.

When I have big emotional issues in the future, I should not go to my parents. I should distract myself.

I should not bond with others when I am mourning.

If I want to get a new toy, all I have to do is act like I feel anguish.

My parents think I can't handle this loss. Maybe they are right.

When children are inhibited from experiencing anguish they rarely learn to embrace, process, and adapt to grief while bonding with others who are mourning the same loss. Instead they learn to isolate from others and distract with external objects, which may become associated with destructive magical thought. This culture emphasizes that it is the parent's job to keep children happy. Therefore, it is easy to understand why caring parents may have a desire to eliminate anguish from their children. It is difficult for parents to see their children experiencing anguish. Although allowing children to experience anguish appears counter to good parenting, the free expression of anguish is necessary when children are mourning.

Purposes of Anguish

Anguish offers children important knowledge and insight. Anguish teaches survivors the essence of the person who is dead. Every little interaction their loved one offered when alive is realized since the death. Every meaningful value reflecting the dead loved one is high-lighted. Through these realizations, children can come to understand the total value of their deceased loved one. Anguish teaches children how much they actually loved the dead person. Anguish also teaches children their own potential for love. Anguish teaches children that without anguish, love would be so easy it would be worthless. With adult support, children may realize that love lost creates anguish.

It is easy to understand that caring and well-intended parents may be enticed to stop their children from feeling anguish. Our culture supports the notion that children should be in a continuous state of happiness and parents feel that cultural pressure. To see a child in anguish is very difficult, but stopping anguish is like trying to stop love. Interfering with the normal grief emotion of anguish is destructive to children's process of mourning, personality development, developing coping mechanisms, and nurturing relationships with adults. Grief therapists and caring adults need to advocate that children not be distracted from their anguish.

PARENT SUGGESTION

Children need simple explanations that they feel anguish (the desperate feeling like something is missing and you cannot get it back) because the person who died is not replaceable and that person was very special. Anguish is connected to love.

Anger

Children experiencing the normal grief emotion of anger, are often angry because their loved one is dead, they are forced to make uncomfortable adjustments, and because they experience constant reminders that their loved one is gone. Children often feel anger when a loved one dies, which is part of normal process of mourning.

Anger can become dysfunctional when children express anger with passive-aggressive reactions. Passive-aggressive anger will be discussed here, not because it is a normal and healthy grief response, but because it is so commonly experienced with children and teenagers. Parents understand passive-aggressive reactions better when they are termed "button pushing." Most children are very adept at button pushing and it is quite common in families. Healthy button pushing usually has the goal of children getting what they want from parents, which is normal and typical. Children pushing parents' buttons is normal and actually a sign of enhanced intelligence. For instance, bright children know which parent they prefer to ask for money, car keys, and special activities. For angry children who are developing a complicated mourning, button pushing usually has the goal of attaining revenge, which is abnormal, not uncommon, and very unhealthy.

Shawn, a fourteen-year-old boy, was at home with his mother when his father, filled with anger and rage, burst into the house. In front of Shawn, his father blamed Shawn's mother for everything that ever went wrong in their marriage. His father left their home and divorced Shawn's mother. After the divorce, Shawn's father rarely visited him. Shawn was very angry about the death of his parents' marriage but he did not realize that was why he was angry. In the depths of Shawn's heart was a realization that he could never let any anger out toward his father because his father had demonstrated that he would leave people. Shawn rarely saw his father, so he did not display any anger toward him for fear that his father would never come back. Instead, Shawn displaced his anger onto the one person he knew would never leave him. In this case the safe person was Shawn's mother. Shawn was an expert in pushing his mother's buttons. Shawn realized that his mother valued Christian beliefs, which was an "easy access" button. As she was proceeding through this crisis, she openly practiced her faith to encourage herself. Shawn loved to push on his mother's religious button. Every evening when they sat down to eat dinner Shawn's mother would say a prayer, which was a routine time when Shawn truly enjoyed pushing her religious button. He would say, "God's a loser! I don't believe in God. I'm not going to church anymore." She would stand up, rant and rave, and act very ungodly. She realized her buttons were being pushed and she felt very out of control. She also realized that her angry fourteen-year-old son was not going to stop pushing her buttons. She asked her therapist what she could do to change this situation. She was advised not to let Shawn know about any other personal buttons she may have and not to respond in the same predictable fashion when he pushes the buttons already unearthed. She considered this advice. When she went home that evening and sat down for dinner, she started to say a prayer. He started to push her buttons but nothing was working. Finally he said to her, "Hey, guess what? I'm going to become a Satanic Worshipper!" She felt the twinge of her religious button being pushed. She resisted her desire to "go off." She looked at him with deep contemplation and finally said to her son who had a deep look of smirk on his face, "OK, why don't we all become Satanic Worshippers. Do you know what they do to their kids!" He never brought it up again.

Shawn's need for revenge, motivated by anger connected to his process of mourning, had a purpose.

THE PURPOSES OF PASSIVE-AGGRESSIVE REACTIONS: BUTTON PUSHING FOR REVENGE

Passive-aggressive reactions have healthy and unhealthy purposes. Bereaved children often feel crippled in their ability to experience empowerment. If a loved one dies, children have no power to bring them back. If parents divorce, children have no power to re-unite their parents. Bereaved children often feel void of empowerment with many of the issues that matter to them. They learn, often by trial and error, that when they say certain phrases or do certain activities, their parents ignite offering children power over their parents' immediate behavior. The power that passive-aggressive behavior offers children is enticing. Passive-aggressive behavior gives unempowered children the illusion of power. However, it is only an illusion because passive-aggressive reactions destroy their reputation and relationships.

Passive-aggressive reactions also give children revenge. Bereaved children feel tremendous hurt and pain. They have been taught that blame is usually assigned to someone when something goes wrong. Bereaved children often conclude that they hurt because someone did something wrong, which justifies their need for revenge.

One positive purpose of passive-aggressive reactions/button pushing is that it may help some children test for safety before expressing intense grief emotions. When children push parents' buttons, children are often testing to see if their parents are stable. When parents' buttons are pushed and parents do not lose control, children may have taken a first step toward intimate communication with their parents. If parents lose control when their bereaved children push their buttons, parents have lost an opportunity for a gradual move toward emotional intimacy with their children.

PARENT SUGGESTION

Angry passive-aggressive reactions from bereaved children are an indicator that grief therapy is needed. The need for revenge that drives children's passive-aggressive reactions is significant, especially when considering that their personality is developing and may be affected by their need for revenge.

Guilt

Healthy guilt is an emotion that makes children feel bad about themselves, not with the intention of destroying children, but to activate self-correction. When children correct themselves by making amends, their guilt is usually alleviated.

In a healthy form, guilt creates action, which leads children to make amends for wrongs they have committed. Fifteen-year-old Amber's last words to her mother were quite nasty as Amber complained and used inappropriate language when her mother refused to let Amber do an activity with her friends. When Amber's mother was killed in a car accident several hours later, Amber felt intense and prolonged guilt. Typically, guilt encourages children to make amends for inappropriate behavior, as the feeling of guilt is not relieved until amends are offered. Amber's mother was dead and amends could not be made to Amber's mother. Guilt also teaches valuable lessons and, in this case, guilt taught Amber that inappropriate language might have permanent effects, especially when it is the last interaction with someone she loves. Amber's guilt would not diminish because Amber believed that she could never make amends to her mother. Amber was taught through grief therapy that she could always make amends to life and include her mother. Amber realized that her mother's favorite charity was a local hospice, as her mother donated time and money to this organization. Amber made amends to life and her mother by offering some of her time and efforts to the same hospice. This brought her closer to her mother's forgiving heart and Amber came to realize that her mother would forgive her. Amber was also asked to recall all of those many times Amber and her mother connected in so many positive ways throughout Amber's life. Amber's recall of these positive connections with her mother helped her to erase the impact of one inappropriate ill-timed interaction. Amber learned significant lessons and felt she had made amends to her mother.

Healthy guilt offers two powerful purposes: 1) Healthy guilt offers children internal direction to make amends. 2) Healthy guilt teaches lessons in life usually in the form, "I will never do that behavior again because it hurts people I care about."

When people experience unhealthy guilt it is a common but not a normal grief emotion. Normal grief emotions serve a productive purpose of maintaining a healthy process of mourning. Unhealthy guilt is often quite manipulative to self and/or others resulting in self-blame and/or scapegoating. Unhealthy guilt also seeks to destroy and it is counter to a healthy process of mourning.

SUMMARY

In summary, consider the brief listing, that the reader can easily refer to, of bereaved children's normal grief emotions and their purposes:

Grief Emotions	Purposes
1. Numb and Stunned Reaction	Inhibits being overwhelmed. Signals unusual event has happened. Braces children to prepare for trauma. Allows objective information gathering. Allows children to find safety before emoting.
2. Commotion	Calls attention to mourning child. Offers a barometer of a need to express grief.
3. Attempts to Re-create and Balancing Denial	Helps children realize the loved one is dead. Helps children realize the significance and uniqueness of the dead person.
4. Anguish	Teaches the full value of the dead loved one. Teaches children how much they actually loved the dead person.
5. Anger	Teaches children that they do not like the adjustments associated with losing the dead person.

6. Passive-Aggressive   Demonstrates a dysfunctional mourning
   Reactions   process.
   (Functional and   – Designed to attain revenge.
   Dysfunctional)   + Tests adults for stability and safety.

7. Guilt   Offers children internal direction to make
                                amends.
                          ' Teaches children lessons in life usually in
                                the form of, "I will never do that
                                behavior again because it hurts people."

PARENTAL SUGGESTION

Parents can learn and memorize the purposes of normal grief
emotions. This knowledge can help parents perceive children's
behavior with greater understanding. Knowing the purposes of
the normal grief emotions also allows supportive parents to offer
grief therapists a more accurate picture of their children's grief
reactions and process of mourning.

The normal grief emotions have individual purposes and their
shared purpose is to keep children on a process of healthy mourning.
When normal grief emotions are inhibited/delayed/eliminated, their
productive purposes are lost. When children who are experiencing
them perceive their normal grief emotions as abnormal, children may
develop in accordance with the model of magical thought, which has the
potential to develop complicated mourning. Consider this first definition of complicated mourning:

*If the purposes of the normal grief emotions are not being served,
there is greater potential for children to develop complicated
mourning.*

Examples:

1) If longing, searching, and pining are inhibited/eliminated,
the potential for dysfunctional denial may increase.

2) If a child is stuck on feeling only one normal grief emotion such as anguish, then the other normal grief emotions are
inhibited/eliminated creating greater potential for complicated
mourning.

Each normal grief emotion has a purpose and together the normal grief emotions promote a healthy process of mourning. When the purposes of the normal grief emotions are inhibited or eliminated, there is greater potential for the development of complicated mourning.

Another component leading children to develop within accordance to the model of magical thought is that children have incomplete cognitive equipment, which they use when attempting to interpret their grief emotions, which is the topic of Chapter 2.

CHAPTER 2

Cognition: The Most Definitive Feature of Children's Grief

It is vital for grief therapists, caregivers, and parents to have full knowledge of how the progression of children's cognitive development affects children's interpretations of grief reactions and their ability to mourn. Cognition is one of the essential differences between children's and adults' mourning processes and can lead children to become confused about their grief reactions. Children have developing, and therefore incomplete cognitive equipment, which can create a greater potential for them to accept destructive magical thought resulting in a process of complicated mourning.

A SPECIAL STATEMENT ABOUT CHILDREN'S COGNITION

Jean Piaget was one of the most recognized and respected theorists in the area of children's cognition. To make Jean Piaget's (1975) concepts practical in the clinical setting, this author offers three usable categories of children's cognition utilizing terms familiar to parents and often utilized by practicing therapists.

1. Basic Skills—The Basic Skills category of cognition includes Jean Piaget's (1975) sensorimotor period. Children with basic skills do not recognize that the world operates with certain rules. Without the ability to recognize the rules of this world, children with basic skills cannot impact their world or psychologically protect themselves from the world. Grief therapists, assisting children in this category of cognition, spend considerable time consulting and educating parents about children's grief reactions.

2. Concrete Thinking—The Concrete Thinking category includes Jean Piaget's (1975) preoperational period and concrete operations period. Children in the Concrete Thinking category eventually and progressively comprehend the rules of this world, but they are very linear in their thought processes and do not creatively impact their world. They have most cognitive skills with the exception of abstract reasoning or they may have early and very immature abstract reasoning. Children with concrete thinking have difficulty perceiving a comprehensive process, such as the life to death cycle and the process of grief. Grief therapists can directly effect change in concrete thinking children by offering more comprehensive insights and options that children cannot attain due to their lack of abstract reasoning.

3. Abstract Reasoning—The Abstract Reasoning category reflects Jean Piaget's (1975) formal operations of cognition. Children with abstract reasoning have a more comprehensive view of the world and greater understanding of the rules of the world. Important to therapists, children with abstract reasoning impact their world with greater intensity, can understand the emotions of others, and perceive their grief and mourning as a comprehensive process.

Much of the discussion of this book includes children within the categories of basic skills, concrete thinking, and abstract reasoning. These three categories of cognition are understandable to parents and are usable to practicing therapists who treat bereaved children.

Cognitive development is so variable among children of the same chronological age, that offering age ranges to categorize cognitive development often assumes normal development. Children are so different in their cognitive development that average ages describing cognition are often inaccurate when applied to individual children. Instead of age ranges, consider the following descriptors of children's cognitive developmental processes and realize that determining the mental age of each bereaved child is more important than the child's chronological age. The cognitive descriptors listed below offer guideposts as to how children may cognitively perceive grief and the process of mourning.

Children's transition from concrete to abstract reasoning is of the utmost importance. Instead of grief therapists' concern about children's age and averages of development, the grief therapist can consider the existence of concrete versus abstract reasoning as an important factor when determining how children think about grief.

To Bond or Not To Bond

Often, when grief therapists counsel grief-stricken, angry teenagers and their parents, this scenario arises. A seventeen-year-old boy was angry and utilized opposition to maintain a detached relationship with his father. This teenage boy's anger was becoming increasingly anti-social as he was dabbling in illegal activity. He was legally forced to go to therapy. The therapist mentioned to the teenager's father that the therapist was concerned that the teenager's anger and use of anger to maintain detachment may be related to the loss of the teenager's mother, who died when the boy was a mere three months old. The father disregarded this idea stating, "My teenager does not *remember* his mother so her death could not be the issue that is influencing his anger." When considering a child's development and its effects, parents rely heavily on the concept of memory. This parent is correct that when his son was three months old the boy did not have the capacity to remember a visual image of his mother or the circumstances of her death. However, this boy did have a basic skill as an infant that could allow his main caregiver's death to impact him within the first several months of life. John Bowlby (1988), in his considerable and impressive research, has found that within the early months of life infants desire one person. "There is abundant evidence that almost every child habitually prefers one person . . . when distressed" (Bowlby, 1988, p. 28). Children, within the early months of life, do not like anything different and want to maintain this same relationship. John Bowlby (1988) suggests this cognitive feature of striving to maintain sameness with this priority relationship within early infancy exists to enhance bonding and maintain continuous contact with the main caregiver. John Bowlby (1988) suggests that an infant's need for sameness is probably a survival skill due to the extreme dependency of the infant. John Bowlby (1979) suggests that when this very early bond between caregiver and infant is broken, the infant will have psychiatric distur-bances that may be life-long. When children who have attachment difficulties are in their elementary school years, they often attempt to mimic emotional bonding by observing others and performing the same behaviors. For example, children of this age may observe people hug-ging and imitate hugging behavior. It is difficult to fake a hug. Children with attachment difficulties will imitate hugging behavior but they find it is difficult to feel emotions attached to their hug, which results in a very superficial hug. As children with attachment problems progress into their adolescence, they often become frustrated with their inability to attach. To maintain detachment they often rely on anger as their major defense, which offers the illusion of power, creates oppositional attitudes and, for some children, results in unacceptable conduct or anti-social behavioral reactions (illegal behavior).

Another basic skill children develop within the early months of life is that they absorb the emotions and tensions of those around them, like a sponge. To demonstrate young children's ability to absorb, the following marital therapy example is offered. A husband and wife were receiving marital therapy for communication issues. When they went to their marital therapy sessions, they always brought their four-month-old baby and usually the father held the baby throughout each session. Children have "built-in" barometers and this four-month-old infant's barometer was going to tell the therapist how well each marital session was progressing. Most marital therapy sessions are one hour and typically each session is divided into three twenty-minute-segments. The first twenty-minute-segment is usually relaxed with spouses commenting on the events of the week. The second twenty-minute-segment is often filled with intense hurts and resentments, which surface creating considerable spousal tension. If the session progresses well, in the last twenty-minute-segment their tension sub-sides as the couple utilizes the skills offered by the therapist. In this case, during the first twenty minutes of each session this four-month-old infant appeared very calm and content in father's arms. As the tension brewed between the adults within the second twenty-minute-segment, this four-month-old infant turned beet red, squirmed, and offered blood-curdling screams. This infant was immediately absorbing the tension of his parents as his cognition was too immature to have developed sophisticated psychological defense mechanisms, that would allow him to fend off his parents' tension. As this infant felt his parents' tension subside in the third twenty-minute-segment, he started to become calm. Infants immediately absorb the emotions and tensions of their parents. Imagine the amount of tension absorbed by children of this very young age when there exists an extremely complicated, dys-functional and tension-filled grief process within their family.

PARENT SUGGESTION

If you have an adolescent who is angry and detached, review the adolescent's first few years of life to determine if the adolescent had any significant loss experiences. If a grief therapist is assist-ing, be sure to inform the grief therapist of any very early loss your child has experienced. Loss experiences, such as the main caregiver dying or the main caregiver having had emotional difficulties (e.g., grief from a loss) during the first few months of a child's life that may inhibit the caregiver's ability to offer quality care, and may have enhanced the development of reactive attachment disorder.

Imitation

Assuming normal childhood development, imitation is the basic skill that usually develops for many children within the first several years of life. Children continue to absorb emotions and, combined with the skill of imitation, they can mimic all the best and worst behavioral reactions of their immediate family. When there is a process of mourning within their family, children of this age have the opportunity to absorb and imitate healing grief reactions, disenfranchised grief, dysfunctional grief reactions, and any other factors present. Absorption and imitation of complicated mourning processes may account for commotion reactions (excessive behavior related to grief) that resemble and are often misdiagnosed as ADHD. Severe commotion reactions may start in the early stages of infancy, as infants do not have the cognitive equipment to develop psychological defenses, especially if complicated mourning is within the family at that time. This early onset is also a criteria often associated with ADHD, which may be the resulting misdiagnosis instead of the correct diagnosis of mourning (commotion), assuming proper assessments are not offered and developmental histories not administered.

Concrete Thinking

As children progress into their pre-school and early elementary school years they start to develop skills that reflect concrete thinking which are cognitive skills that are advanced enough to be utilized in education and counseling. A leading skill that is developed within children throughout this developmental period is memory. Children also have experiences to remember as they progress and explore their world. With memory and experiences, children can start to anticipate. For example, a parent says to a concrete thinking five-year-old girl, "On Saturday we are all going to a birthday party." This five-year-old girl has had the previous experience of going to a birthday party and she can remember this experience. She recalls enjoying birthday cake, new presents, playing games, many kids, and fun. Her memory and previous experience now starts to affect her current emotions and behavior. She becomes emotionally excited about the upcoming birthday party and she starts exhibiting excited behavior by jumping up and down for joy. Consider a different scenario. Her mother tells this same little five-year-old girl that on Saturday they are going to visit her cousin Sabrina. Sabrina is four years older and a very big and mean girl. Sabrina always enjoys beating up this five-year-old girl whenever they get together. The five-year-old girl recalls these beatings and can anticipate her oncoming beating as Saturday approaches. Her recollections and anticipation start to affect her emotions and her behavior. She feels the emotions of vulnerability, apprehension, and fear. When Saturday arrives her behavior is affected as she avoids getting into the car and withdraws into her room.

The two lessons of this example are:

Assuming no mental disorders, neurological impairment, and/or chemical usage, all emotions have messages.

Memory and experiences help children to anticipate, which can affect children's emotions and behavior.

This five-year-old girl was able to recall previous experiences, which helped her anticipate these future Saturday events. In anticipating these events, her emotions were reflected in her behavior. Her emotions offered her and her family messages:

I am excited about the birthday party and I can't wait to go.

I fear my cousin Sabrina and I don't want to go.

There is another cognitive skill that develops within children during this developmental period. Children with concrete thinking can start to create pictures in their mind. The phrase "mini-movies in your head" helps concrete thinking children understand the tool of a remembered image.

With the combination of these cognitive skills (memory, anticipation, and imagery), concrete thinking children are capable of making simple connections and responding to therapy, especially therapy that incorporates action and activities.

THE STORY OF HEATHER

Heather was a five-year-old girl who was quite grief-stricken when she came into a counseling center. Her magical thought was obvious from her body language, facial expressions, tone of voice, and verbalizations. Her magical thought was, "I have no power in my life so I can do nothing to help myself." There were two events that convinced her that she had no power in her life. She was very emotionally close to her grandfather and he lived a few blocks away. He was dying. She tried everything she could to stop him from dying, but as he deteriorated she eventually realized that he was dying. Adding to the complexity of this situation, her parents were getting a divorce. Just as she had done in her grandfather's case, she did everything she could to stop her parents from getting a divorce. She saw her father move out of the house and she realized that the divorce could not be stopped. In her mind, she had failed twice. Due to her interpretation of these losses, she convinced herself that she lacked control and power in her life. Despite this negative conclusion, Heather compensated by utilizing a very important skill found in most children; she created her own devices to make herself feel better. A favorite question of therapists and caregivers for bereaved children is, "What have you done to help make yourself feel better?" She answered this question, "I used to go to my girlfriend's house next door to play." Used to? When she was asked why she did not go there anymore she replied, "Well because of the neighbor mother." Referring to her friend's mother, she told stories of how intrusive the neighbor mother was with continuous probing and nosy questioning. The neighbor mother intruded upon Heather with questions such as, "Has your Dad been served with papers by the Sheriff yet?" and "Have your Grandpa's kidneys failed?" After experiencing the neighbor mother's constant intrusive questions, Heather remembered the intrusions. Using her memory of these experiences Heather could anticipate her neighbor mother's intrusiveness, which created emotions for Heather with associated behavior. Heather felt emotionally vulnerable when intruded upon by the many questions of the neighbor mother, which led Heather to avoidance behavior. Heather discontinued visiting her five-year-old neighbor friend. A quick solution would have been to advise Heather's mother to talk to the intrusive neighbor mom to stop these intrusions. This solution would have missed a very important opportunity to assist with the development of Heather's personal empowerment by addressing her magical thought, "I have no power in my life so I can do nothing to help myself." Heather's mother resolving this situation for Heather would not enhance Heather's personal feelings of empowerment. With the cognitive skills mentioned above (memory, anticipation, imaging), action-focused techniques could be utilized to impinge upon Heather's destructive magical thought, "I have no power in my life so I can do nothing to help myself," by demonstrating that she does have power. Heather's grief therapist told Heather that they were going to perform a play like in a theater (concrete way of describing a psychodrama) and that Heather would be the director who would tell everyone what to do. Putting her in the director position offered Heather one element of empowerment. The grief therapist told Heather that the grief therapist would play the role of the intrusive neighbor mother, Heather's mother would play her five-year-old friend, and Heather would play herself. The grief therapist asked Heather to go through the counseling office and find props that the grief therapist could wear that would make the grief therapist look like the intrusive neighbor mother in Heather's eyes. She circulated the counseling office and returned with a very hairy wig and a mask that had a very long nose. She instructed the grief therapist to wear these props. In Heather's view the grief therapist's garb was the neighbor mother. The grief therapist asked Heather to tell the grief therapist (as the intrusive neighbor mother) and to tell her mother (playing her five-year-old friend) exactly what to do when the intrusive neighbor mother asks these many intrusive questions. To the smallest detail, Heather instructed the grief therapist on how to be intrusive and offered the many questions that the neighbor mother had used to persistently badger her. In this performance, Heather demonstrated that she tried to make an adjustment to these intrusions by turning away from the neighbor mother. She directed the grief therapist (playing the neighbor mother) to be more intrusive by standing between Heather and her friend and continuing the barrage of questions. Heather identified stresses within her five-year-old friend by telling Heather's mother (who was playing her five-year-old friend) how to act when the neighbor mother was intrusive. By directing this play, Heather offered a host of dysfunctional dynamics at the neighbor's house that could now be addressed in therapy. If a grief therapist had to rely only on Heather's verbalizations without action-focused techniques to gather this information from this five-year-old girl, the dialog might have sounded like this:

Grief Therapist: "Heather, how have you been since your Grandfather is dying?"
Heather: "OK."
Grief Therapist: "Well Heather, how are you doing with Mom and Dad's divorce?"
Heather: "Fine."

Now the grief therapist has an entire therapy hour left! A very long therapy hour!

When Heather was asked to use action-focused techniques, she was able to offer a rich array of responses that were workable in treatment. Children experiencing the development of options in therapy that help them to adjust to their environment, will usually want to come back to see the therapist to do more work, as children see the immediate effects and great value of the sessions that they appreciate.

Action-focused techniques coupled with Heather's concrete reasoning can now be developed to offer possible solutions for Heather to help her regain her feelings of empowerment in this situation. It was suggested to Heather that she could play with her friend again if she could develop ways to effectively handle the intrusions of the neighbor mother. To prime Heather's thinking, her mother and the grief therapist offered suggestions that they could all practice together. Eventually, Heather offered several ideas of her own. Developing one of Heather's ideas gave Heather another element of empowerment. Children who think concretely will often create easy-to-remember one or two-step plans. One of her ideas was excellent because it was simple enough for her to recall easily and offered her assertiveness without passivity or aggression. Together they all agreed it was the best plan and they actively rehearsed this simple plan many times. After the rehearsal, Heather was instructed to make a mini movie (image) of this plan in her memory so she could rehearse it in her mind. She learned that she could take this plan with her, which offered another element of empowerment. Heather was instructed to play this "mini movie" in her mind several times before going to visit her friend, which offered Heather anticipation. She finally went back to her friend's house to play. The neighbor mother immediately became intrusive directing probing and painful questions at Heather. Heather recalled the well-rehearsed plan and performed it. Heather walked over to the telephone and dialed it. She lifted the phone to the neighbor mother and said, "If you have any questions about Grandpa dying and Mom and Dad getting divorced, you can ask my Mom." Heather learned the following lessons:

- Although Heather could not stop her grandfather from dying or her parents from divorcing, Heather realized that she did have the power to adjust to her environment. She found a way to play with her friend.
- Heather could utilize her emotions (apprehension and vulnerability) as a signal. Her emotions sent her the message that she needed to develop an assertive plan of action, instead of using dysfunctional passive withdrawal.

Concrete thinking children are very effective in using action-focused techniques because action-focused techniques are concrete rehearsals of concrete plans of action. More examples of children's mourning process and action-focused techniques will be offered in Chapter 5, "Action Focused Techniques to Eliminate Destructive Magical Thought."

PARENT SUGGESTION

Parents can greatly assist the therapeutic process and empowerment issues for their bereaved children, if parents offer the grief therapist issues that need solutions. Parents can describe their children's day-to-day activities and events that need solutions that can be refined with practice and rehearsal.

WHY IS IT EASY FOR CHILDREN WITH CONCRETE THOUGHT PROCESSES TO DEVELOP MAGICAL THOUGHT?

Next is a discussion of how concrete thinking children do not understand the abstract concept of death, resulting in them developing magical thought about death and grief. Concrete thinking children are learning the rules of this world but their thought processes are immature and inexperienced, allowing easy development of magical thought. Concrete thinking children have a tendency to accept and maintain inaccurate assumptions, promoting magical thoughts about death and grief:

- Concrete thinking children have limited ability to understand or perceive a process such as the life-and-death cycle. Concrete thinking children only live in the here-and-now, with memory of the immediate past, and very little concept of a future. One example of not being able to see a process is when young children are often asked by adults, "What do you want to be when you grow up"? Children immediately offer their favorite answers which often reflects what they have seen in their environment such as policeman, fireman, teacher, nurse, etc. Although young children readily know what their favorite answer is to that question, they actually have no idea how to engage in the process to becoming a fireman, policeman, nurse, etc. Because they think concretely, they cannot perceive a continuous process of development. They can only see the here and now. Because they can only see the here and now, they truly believe that nothing will ever change. If someone they know dies, children do not perceive the death as the result of the life-and-death cycle, the death just happened. Because children are cognitively inclined to believe nothing will ever change, they also cannot conceive that they will ever die.

- Concrete thinking children are cognitively inclined to define all situations as happy or sad and good or bad. If a concrete thinking child has a family member die and everyone expresses sadness, the child will define this death experience as bad because sad equals bad. This simple concrete cognition can work against children. Although there are excellent media and movies available to help discuss death and grief with children, there is a segment of commercial movies that may reinforce the distorted "good or bad" concept. For example, in one of my adolescent groups, I suggested that the group randomly pick a violent Hollywood movie with a specific goal other than just watching violence. The teenagers were asked to count the number of deaths that occurred in this particular movie. They became frustrated counting so many deaths that after having finished only two-thirds of the movie, they counted 340 deaths. When young children mourning the death of a loved one are excessively exposed to very violent movies with a theme that suggests that only bad people die, the solidification of children's destructive magical thoughts may occur. For example, if a child concludes that only bad people die, the child may develop this one of many possible magical thoughts, "If I want to stay alive, I better be perfectly good."

  Another way the "good or bad" concept often enters the thoughts of concrete thinking children is in the form of bereaved children's questions similar to this, "Did Grandpa die because he did something bad?" If this question goes unasked and/or unanswered and children conclude that people could die if they are bad, children may develop a variety of destructive magical thoughts based on being perfectly good or becoming like the violent hero of a movie, in order to stay alive.

  I better be perfectly good so I won't die.

  I better be in control (like the violent hero of movies) so I won't die.

- Children with concrete thinking believe that death is not final and that their magical thoughts can stop a loved one from dying and/or bring back a dead loved one. This belief is responsible for the development of considerably destructive magical thought within young children in regard to the issue of death. Concrete thinking children cannot perceive a process such as the life-and-death cycle or the process of a continuous stream of mourning. The egocentricity of children often leads them to believe that they are responsible for a loved one's death and children surmise that they should also have the power to fix the situation.

> It is my fault Mom died because I touched Mom when I was sick and then she got sick and died. If I have that much power, I should be able to bring her back to life.

PARENT SUGGESTION

Parents can be quite effective in helping children realize that their dead loved one is not coming back. It is helpful for children, who think concretely, to have concrete experiences. It is important for children to go to visitations and funerals to actually see their dead loved ones. If parents have religious beliefs that discourage viewing the body, attending the rituals of most religions help children recognize the reality of the death of a loved one.

- Children with concrete thinking apply power to their parents that does not exist. Parents are perceived, by concrete thinking children, as having the ability to do anything. For example, when a very young girl scrapes her knee, she may run to a parent and the parent hugs her. The pain from her wound seems to magically disappear. This inaccurate perception, of parents' power-base, can complicate children's process of mourning. A child could conclude:

> Mom and Dad, if you are so powerful bring my dead brother back.

> Mom and Dad, make the pain of my grief go away.

A concrete thinking child may conclude that if the child performs a certain set of behaviors (perfectionism, aggressive control, whining, etc.), the child's parents will make his or her pain of grief go away. Children's magical thoughts, based on concrete cognition (parents are all powerful), can lead children to a dysfunctional set of behaviors (perfectionism, aggressive control, whining, etc.), which may confuse and perplex parents.

In summary, children's concrete cognition is susceptible to misinterpretation allowing simple magical thoughts that may lead them to an unhealthy and complicated mourning process. Concrete thinking does not naturally allow children to realize the abstract concept that their life is constantly changing and that they are on a life-to-death cycle. The exercise described below is helpful in assisting concrete thinking children to understand the abstract concept that grief is a process. It is an exercise that can be used in the classroom to educate children about grief, as a therapeutic group activity, and as a training exercise for caregivers (see Figure 1).

With a group of children, the adult leader holds up a piece of normal sized writing paper with the word "DEATH" written on it. While holding the paper up in a still position, the adult leader starts to slowly walk in a straight line and say, "There was a time in my life when death never affected me. I had never experienced a death and death had no effect on me."

Figure 1. The Paper Exercise: "The Adult Leader."

"Then when I was eight years old my brother died (now the leader flops the paper labeled "DEATH" around in an uncontrollable manner, still slowly walking a straight line). I thought to myself, "I wish it was back like it was before" but that did not help. Then I thought, "I will pretend that this is not happening" (paper keeps flopping around uncontrollably while leader walks slowly in a straight line). That did not help. Well maybe if I act perfect the grief (paper) will go away (paper keeps flopping). "No, that did not help. Anger gives me power so maybe if I am angry enough, the grief will go away (paper keeps flopping). That did not help."

"Maybe I need to get some help from others." (The leader asks one of the children to rip some of the paper away. The paper continues to flop but not as much.) "I need to get more help." (The leader has another child rip off some paper, and then another until there is only a small piece left. The paper is now small and no longer flopping.)

"Now maybe I can work on it, too." (While continuing to walk slowly in a straight line, the leader rips off a little bit of the paper.) "Now I think I can manage it." (The leader holds the small paper that is left, looks at it, puts it in his or her pocket, takes it out to look at it again, and then puts it away in his or her pocket.) "It's not completely gone, but it feels better!"

The most important part of any technique is the discussion it creates. With this exercise the adult leader could guide the discussion to cover the following issues:

1. Grief never goes away, but it can become manageable.
2. Grief does not get better unless we work on it together.
3. Magical thoughts will not make grief and the process of mourning better. For example, "If I am perfect, my grief will go away" has been demonstrated not to work with this exercise.
4. Slowly walking the straight line allows the leader to concretely demonstrate a process. At one point in the line, the process of mourning was out of control. By working on it together (by asking others to rip pieces from this paper), it became apparent that at some point on the line, the process of mourning eventually became manageable.

This exercise is utilizing children's concrete thinking by demonstrating the abstract process of mourning with a concrete image. These concrete images (walking the line and the paper) will help children to understand where they are in the process of their mourning. In the beginning of the straight line that the adult leader was walking, the adult leader offered a symbol of mourning that was out of control (flopping the paper). As the adult leader was walking a straight line and got help from others, the mourning process eventually became more manageable and the symbol (paper) also became manageable.

When the adult leader sees improvement with certain grief issues for children, the adult leader can refer back to this exercise as a concrete expression of improvement. For example, an adult leader could offer, "Oh, I think you are here with this issue" (referring to that point on the line where the paper is smaller, suggesting the issue is now more manageable).

On issues where there has not been much progress, the adult leader can refer to the point on the line where the paper is much larger. For example the adult leader could say, "On this other issue I think you are here" (referring to that point on the line where the paper is larger, suggesting that the issue is not at the point of being manageable yet).

THE ONSET OF ABSTRACT REASONING

The onset of abstract reasoning will change the perception of death and grief for bereaved children. One of the first concerns, for grief therapists and parents, is a need to assess abstract reasoning to determine its existence in the bereaved children they are attempting to assist. The grief therapist can use the following academic and interactive techniques to assess the presence of abstract reasoning.

Academic Technique

Most verbal intelligence tests have a Similarities subtest that asks children to describe how two concepts are similar. Children's responses to Similarities subtests can differentiate between children's concrete and abstract thought. Consider the following examples:

Concepts	Concrete Response	Abstract Response
House and Tent	"They have roofs."	"Dwellings to live in."
Bike and Car	"They have tires."	"Types of transportation."
Flower and Tree	"They have roots."	"Forms of life."
Radio and TV	"They have knobs."	"Types of communication."

Children with concrete thinking focus on one small aspect that two objects have in common. Children with abstract thought processes tend to categorize objects, suggesting a higher level of thought.

Interactive Technique

Many years ago I bought my first computer for report writing and business. I decided to use the computer with the children in therapy by offering a menu of games that we could play together. The mutual fun of playing these games allowed us to finish therapy sessions on a positive note. One of the first children I played a computer game with, taught me that it may be possible to assess children's abstract thought processes with competitive computerized games. As I was playing computerized basketball with an eight-year-old boy, I realized that my fine psychomotor skills were much more aged than his movements—a built in disadvantage. The score was 108 to 6 in his favor. As he was playing he was fairly stress free until he happened to take a glimpse of me. Apparently, I appeared very stressed as I was attempting to shoot baskets. He read my body language and realized that I was stressed. He looked at me as if to say, "Poor old guy." He then started to let me make baskets and I started to relax. What happened? Concrete thinking children without abstract reasoning may mimic empathy, but children with abstract reasoning utilize real empathy. This eight-year-old boy read my emotional state. He incorporated his reading of my emotional state into his thoughts. He eventually felt my emotional reaction as I was struggling with this computer game, and he started to make behavioral adjustments to accommodate me. His level of empathy and ability to read my reactions required abstract reasoning. This activity is a wonderful interactive tech-nique that assesses children's abstract reasoning. Children without abstract reasoning typically do not realize their competitor's emo-tional state. Children with a small level of abstract reasoning, creating a small level of empathy, will let their competitor make baskets to catch up. Children with a higher level of abstraction, resulting in a higher level of empathy, realize that their com-petitors need to win an occasional game to feel encouraged. What is also advantageous about this technique is that if the therapist is over thirty years of age, losing does not have to be faked as the natural deterioration of fine psychomotor skills is obvious. I *think* that is an advantage!

It is helpful to offer both the academic and interactive techniques to determine children's levels of abstract reasoning. Children do not seem to mind the academic technique, as they often have academic questions at school. By offering both assessments, an examiner may find that some children perform well on the academic assessment of abstraction, but appear to have very little empathy as shown through the interactive game playing. This discovery may sug-gest the existence of abstract reasoning with personality factors nega-tively affecting their concern for empathy. These personality factors may also impact on children's mourning processes and how they func-tion in their family.

PARENT SUGGESTION

An assessment of children's abstract reasoning needs to be administered by a qualified examiner. Parents can request that a school psychologist or learning disabilities teacher assess children's abstract reasoning. A psychologist in private practice can also administer a complete cognitive assessment in approximately one hour.

ABSTRACT REASONING CHANGES THE PLAYING FIELD

As children's abstract reasoning evolves, enlightenment occurs as children come to realize, "Everyone I know is going to die." When children are concrete with their thinking, they believe that nothing will ever change. Abstract reasoning allows children to realize that they are in a process which has a beginning and an end. Children with early abstract reasoning are leaving the concrete idea of happenstance and starting to develop the initial realization of the process of the life-and-death cycle.

In my grief seminars I often ask the audience if they recall as a child, the first time they realized that everyone is eventually going to die. Usually half of the audience will recall when this realization occurred. When I ask how many people talked to their parents about this profound realization when it occurred in childhood, very few respond affirmatively. The realization that everyone is going to die is an extraordinary insight that most children rarely discuss with others. Why? Abstract reasoning has a very strong effect on children's emotions. For a concrete thinking child, every issue is simply happy or sad, good or bad. For a child with abstract thinking, emotions are advanced well beyond happy or sad and good or bad. With the onset of abstract reasoning, more comprehensive emotions develop which include happiness, contentment, irritability, embarrassment, humiliation, betrayal, hopelessness, and many more. Emotions have a greater impact on children with abstract reasoning, which ultimately impacts on their behavior. For example, a concrete thinking child may be perfectly comfortable at a visitation or funeral, exploring the funeral home, casket, and asking many questions. Older children with early abstract reasoning often feel more restricted with their movements at the funeral home, due to their increased awareness that they could be potentially embarrassed or humiliated.

PARENT SUGGESTION

Once parents have ascertained that their children have abstract reasoning, parents can have a conversation about this new insight that often accompanies the early development of abstract reasoning. This type of conversation can start to create comfort between parents and children when discussing life-and-death issues. In fact, this conversation is as important as talking to children about sexuality.

Another emotional factor that develops with abstract reasoning is children's new feeling that death and everything associated with death is frightening. It is beneficial for caregivers assisting bereaved children to try to recall their own frightening feelings regarding death. I can recall one Saturday morning when I was fourteen years old, my favorite uncle picked me up to go to his ranch, as he did every Saturday morning. On this particular Saturday morning he stopped at a local funeral home. He had a friend who owned a funeral home and in those years caskets came in large wooden boxes, which he said were perfect containers for oats for his horses. As we walked into the funeral home I noticed something that I did not expect—two dead people. Immediately I felt frightened. I said to my uncle, "There are dead people over there." He replied with a slight smile, "That's because we are in a funeral home." I could not wait to leave. I quickly put the boxes in the back of the truck and waited in the cab of the truck. Despite my intense desire to leave the funeral home, seeing the dead bodies peaked my interest. I asked him a question that children at this level of cognitive development often have, "What do they do to those dead bodies at the funeral home to prepare them for the funeral?" He was not comfortable with this question and changed the subject. When we arrived at the ranch another old uncle happened to be there. I asked him the same question. He told several incredible stories of what they do to the bodies at the funeral home. Having more Irish than he needed, many of his stories were laced with magical thought and were the result of purely exaggerated story telling. That night the other uncle who owned the ranch was killed in a car accident. Two days later when I was arriving at the funeral home for my dead uncle's visitation, the story-telling uncle was waiting at the entrance of the funeral home. He wanted me to know that all of his stories were exaggerations. He was cleaning up my distortions about death and the funeral home, which is an excellent function of the caring adults assisting children who are capable of abstract reasoning. The caring adults can offer abstract thinking children a tour of the funeral home to help children "clean up" their distortions of the funeral home and death by offering the truthful reality. Children with abstract reasoning are at an opportune time for this potential "clean up," because of the quality of questions they will ask when touring a funeral home.

The media can also influence children who have frightening concepts of death and the funeral home. Often the only image of the funeral home children have is what they see in Hollywood movies. Movies geared toward pre-teens and teens, that have a funeral home in the movie, often emphasize the feeling of fright. Typically those movies have funeral homes with crypts, walking dead, murderers, buried-alive victims, and other craziness. Children with early abstract reasoning often feel frightening feelings about death. When the concept of fright is reinforced with bizarre media and no caregiver has helped correct these distortions, then frightening feelings and destructive magical thoughts regarding death and the funeral home may develop. With a tour of the funeral home, children can ask questions and look in back rooms so their imagination does not create and reflect fright. Honest facts will correct frightening distortions and destructive magical thought regarding death and funeral issues.

More complete and comprehensive abstract thinking does not necessarily inhibit distorted and destructive magical thought. Indeed, abstract reasoning often embellishes magical thought, making it more complicated. For example, a concrete thinking child may conclude that he or she can stop a dying person from dying or bring back a person who has died. An abstract thinking child could expand on these thoughts concluding that there is life after death. The abstract thinking child may further conclude that the child can re-unite with the dead loved one by committing suicide.

Some abstract reasoning children will use their newfound cognitive skills with good intention, but their use may yield very destructive consequences. A sixteen-year-old girl, with well-developed empathy, wanted to help her bereaved parents after the accidental death of her sister. Instead of processing her grief reactions through the tasks of healthy mourning, she utilized her abstract reasoning and ability to create magical thought by concluding she could magically take away her parents' painful grief.

If I act like my sister, my parents won't miss her so much.

This sixteen-year-old girl, harboring this destructive magical thought, started to lose her own personality.

Abstract reasoning can make destructive magical thought much more complicated, even though the magical thought is often founded on simplistic black and white thinking. An example of this process is an adult who is intellectually narcissistic. An intellectually narcissistic adult is a very bright person who has the capacity to think abstractly in many intellectual areas. This adult may be able to think abstractly about mathematics, computer science, physics, models, theories, and much more. Despite these gifts, the adult may choose to not abstract about grief emotions by developing destructive magical thought. An individual with intellectual narcissism may harbor the magical thought that the adult can handle emotions by using intellect only, which of course is the defense mechanism of intellectualization. The adult also harbors the simplistic cognitive distortion that the adult is right and everyone offering advice about the process of mourning is wrong. The result is that the adult never embraces or processes grief. Instead the adult intellectualizes grief emotions and takes the position that the adult is right and everyone attempting to assist is wrong.

ADOLESCENCE
ABSTRACT THOUGHT UNLEASHED

Most teenagers who have developed normal abstract thinking have the cognitive ability to realize that everyone will eventually die and that death is irreversible. These realizations are muddied, as when teenagers are developing throughout their adolescent years they have Captain James T. Kirk Syndrome. Captain James T. Kirk was invincible. He was placed in dangerous situations where most people would have been killed, but not Captain James T. Kirk. Teenagers have this same feeling of invincibility. Although most teenagers have the cognitive ability to understand that death is universal and irreversible, they still feel invincible when considering death. This cognitive idiosyncrasy of adolescence may occur because of where teenagers are positioned in their general development. Individuals over the age of forty years also understand that death is universal and irreversible. However, forty-year-old people also experience something that most teenagers have not—physical deterioration. Physical deterioration offers many reminders for older adults of the progression of the life-and-death cycle. Most teenagers are experiencing rapid growth including emotional development, cognitive enhancement, physical development, increased territories, independence, social variety, etc. Therefore, it is understandable that teenagers, having felt no deterioration, would view their own personal death as a fearful interruption or an enemy. Teenagers perceive that death is for others; they are invincible, like Captain James T. Kirk.

Teenagers who have the capacity for abstract reasoning entertain religious and spiritual beliefs more prominently than children with concrete thinking do. When mourning, teenagers may consider their family's religion, rebel against their family's religion, and/or create their own spirituality. Most religions and spirituality offer assistance with processing healthy mourning as well as another outlet for communication of grief issues. However, there are many dangers. Teenagers with abstract reasoning may utilize religion and spirituality to help process with healthy mourning or they may distort religion and spirituality by using magical thought, adding destructive elements.

PARENT SUGGESTION

If your family shares religious beliefs, have a cautious ear when children are discussing their beliefs about how they believe their religion works. Children often hold the simple belief that God will automatically make everything better. When God does not quickly make everything better, children can become very angry with God, which can easily transfer to parents.

One angry teenager, who was mourning the murder of his girlfriend, developed a spirituality that he believed released him from his anger, but in fact, it led him to become quite self-destructive. He developed a belief in reincarnation. He believed that he and his girlfriend were soulmates and that they would be together in a future life. He decided that to get his girlfriend back, that he would kill himself to quicken this process. The distortions he placed upon spirituality helped him manufacture destructive magical thought.

In another example, a teenage girl, who was raised as a Catholic, created a destructive magical thought based on her Catholic beliefs. She concluded that if she killed herself she would go to purgatory and then eventually she would be re-united with her father in heaven. This teenager distorted the intent of her religious beliefs with her own destructive magical thought. Neither reincarnation nor Catholicism advocates self-destruction. However, as in this and the previous example, teenagers have used and distorted a variety of religious and spiritual beliefs by adding their own destructive magical thought, potentially resulting in their own destruction.

Religious and spiritual issues with death and grief can be complicated for caregivers. If 100 people were asked to describe their religious or spiritual beliefs, they would probably offer 100 different views. People in the same religion will often focus on different beliefs or principles. These different religious and spiritual perspectives create potential complications for caregivers working with a variety of children and families from various backgrounds. Often clergy have noted that when they are assisting bereaved families, it has been helpful to be perceived as a clergy person, and at other times it has not been helpful as family members may have inaccurate preconceived notions of the clergy. For caregivers in the public school system, a liability lawsuit may occur if they discuss religion and spirituality with bereaved school children, due to the concerns for separation of church and state. For grief therapists working with bereaved families with wide varieties of religions and spirituality, a nice exact fit between grief therapist's religion and family's religion is not always feasible and rarely occurs. There is a role a grief therapist can assume no matter what religion and spirituality the family may believe. The grief therapist can guide anyone in any religion or spirituality by helping them to inhibit the application of destructive magical thought to their religion or spirituality.

The two previous examples demonstrate the destructiveness of magical thought that children may try to attribute to their religion or spirituality. Healthy magical thought reflecting the tasks of healthy mourning could also be utilized with religion and spirituality. One task of mourning is to convert the relationship with the deceased from one of presence to a relationship of memory (Wolfelt, 1988). In a healthy example of utilizing religious beliefs, consider a family who believes in the concept of heaven, reminiscing about a dead loved one. One of the qualities that they did not like about their dead loved one was that he was so compulsively perfectionistic in his organization that he was often irritating to everyone around him. As his family reminisces, his son says, "Dad was so irritating when he was compulsively organizing. I can just see him compulsively arranging clouds and telling angels where to sit in heaven." This religious sharing coupled with a religious concept (heaven) and a positive magical thought of what heaven is like, allows this family to admit to the dead loved one's faults and offers an accurate recollection of what it was like to be with their compulsively perfectionistic father. An accurate memory of the dead loved one is consistent with the tasks of healthy mourning.

It is important for caregivers to consider their role very well, before addressing spiritual and religious issues with bereaved children and their families. To define this role requires a thorough understanding of the caregivers own spirituality, acceptance of others and their cultures, and a working knowledge of the model of magical thought.

Because most teenagers have developing abstract cognitive skills, they have empathy, which can be used to feel what others are feeling and to realize what is important to others. It is not uncommon for normal, non-bereaved teenagers to use empathy to push parental buttons in order to get what they want. Most teenagers will know which parent to ask for use of the car, money, or when they want a "yes" for an activity. Angry bereaved teenagers will use the skill of empathy to attain passive-aggressive revenge. A sixteen-year-old boy felt intense anger with his family. He was at home with his father when his mother came home and blamed his father for the death of their fourteen-year-old daughter. They divorced, and the father retained custody of his sixteen-year-old boy. The boy felt tremendous anger and rage, but he would not let any of his anger out toward his mother. He did not want to lose his mother, as his mother demonstrated that she would leave. The only safe person to direct his anger toward was his father. He continually pushed his father's buttons until his father would explode. This reaction was very enticing to this boy. This boy was mourning and felt little empowerment so when he pushed buttons in adults and they lost control, he felt powerful. What was he doing? Teenagers (and younger children) often push buttons to determine safe ground. When a teenager pushes an adult's button and the adult remains stable, the teenager has taken his first steps to talk intimately with the adult. The adult's stability offers safe ground for the teenager. When button pushing does not attain safe ground, the teenager seeks empowerment. The feeling of empowerment the teenager experiences when the button-pushed adult has a temper tantrum is enticing, irresistible, and actively sought. Adults need to demonstrate stability when their buttons are pushed. To ensure that adults do not have temper tantrums when their buttons are pushed, it is helpful if adults have their reactions planned and rehearsed.

SUMMARY

Children have incomplete cognitive equipment because their brain is in a process of development. It is important for parents and clinicians to understand the tendencies of children to develop inaccurate conclusions about death and grief experiences, due to children's cognitive development. This chapter offered parents and clinicians the realization that very young children can be effected by the process of mourning, even though they do not visually recall the person who died or the grief reactions of other family members. Young children's cognition offers basic skills designed for children to absorb and imitate all the dysfunction and/or functional reactions of their bereaved parents and older siblings. With the development of concrete thinking and abstract reasoning, children are learning the rules of the universe and as their cognition develops their understanding improves. Although children's cognition improves as it develops, it is new and inexperienced resulting in children and teenagers having a tendency to create inaccurate conclusions about life, death, and grief. Children's inaccurate conclusions about life, death, and grief may lead to the development of destructive magical thought, guiding children into a process of complicated mourning.

CHAPTER 3

The Model of Magical Thought

It is necessary to have an understanding of children's normal grief emotions and cognitive development in order to discuss and utilize the Model of Magical Thought. Although there are many avenues for children to develop complicated mourning, children's cognition is the focus of this model. From discussion within Chapter 2 (the section on cognition), it is obvious that children have incomplete cognitive equipment and when coupled with grief emotions, children have great potential for creating inaccurate conclusions which promotes destructive magical thought. Parents and grief therapists can work together to help children eliminate destructive magical thought and to advocate the utilization of the tasks of healthy mourning.

The Model of Magical Thought is one spoke in a very large wheel. The large wheel includes authors who have offered the tasks of healthy mourning, types of complicated mourning, cognitive development, and an array of creative treatment strategies. Having all of this information, I have often wondered how to determine the current point of clinical treatment when spending a therapeutic hour with a young client? How does a grief therapist determine the clinical point of treatment at the time the grief therapist is counseling a child? When a grief therapist searches for and identifies a child's destructive magical thought, the grief therapist is determining the child's current clinical point of treatment.

WHAT IS MAGICAL THOUGHT?

Magical Thought Defined

Magical thought is a child's inaccurate conclusion(s) regarding a loss experience, resulting in the child believing that he or she is responsible for the loss experience and needs to fix the loss experience.

49

Magical thought may lead a child to believe that he or she has developed a method of mourning, but he or she has actually developed an unhealthy and complicated process of mourning. Children have incomplete cognitive equipment, which offers great potential for children to create inaccurate conclusions about major and traumatic events in their life. Children's inaccurate conclusions are often founded on their own misinterpretations or acceptance of inaccurate information, given to them by others about loss experiences and the process of mourning. Magical thought can generate at any point within the mourning process and divert children from the tasks of healthy mourning. Children's acceptance of destructive magical thought, resulting from loss experiences, can become a power-based catalyst for dysfunctional behavioral reactions, the development of destructive defense mechanisms, and (for some children) the creation of potentially permanent personality disorders.

Jean Piaget (1979) discusses young children who do not completely understand the rules of this world can create magical reasoning, believing they have an impact on their world, which is not real. Magical reasoning is similar to magical thought as magical thought also maintains that children believe they have an impact on the world, which is not real. Magical thought is different than Piaget's (1979) magical reasoning as magical thought is not exclusive to young children and a certain developmental period of cognition. Magical thought is an inaccurate system of thought that can impact children's process of mourning at any age, creating one or a combination of many types of complicated mourning.

Consider this "grief due to death" example:

A seven-year-old girl is sick. This sick girl hugs her grandfather when he comes to visit. Her grandfather has a heart attack and dies. This girl concludes, "I was sick and I touched Grandpa and he got sick and died. It is my fault that Grandpa died." This girl later concludes that if she is perfectly good, grandfather will come back, which initiates a pattern of behavior driving her to be compulsively good.

Magical thought can effect other types of loss. Consider this "grief due to divorce" example of magical thought:

An eight-year-old girl's parents have argued intensely over many years about every issue. The girl feels the tension of their arguments, but has effectively learned to "tune out" the words of their arguments. She no longer hears their arguments. Because her parents argue about everything, they eventually argue about her. Only when she hears her name mentioned in their arguments does she listen. This process may continue for months or years until her parents finally decide to divorce. When her parents announce that they are getting divorced, her inaccurate conclusion creates the magical thought, which offers this power-based conclusion, "They were always arguing about me, so I am the reason they are getting divorced. I have the power to make them want to divorce." This first element of power with her magical thought advocates that she has the power to cause her parents' divorce. A second element of power arises when she concludes, "I have the power to fix this situation. I have the power to stop this divorce." This second element of power, acting as a catalyst, will start to generate observable behavior.

Magical thought offers children a double power-based system acting as a catalyst for dysfunctional behaviors, founded on their incomplete cognitive equipment. The Model of Magical Thought offers children three forms of power-based catalysts.

Power-Based Catalysts of Magical Thought

A power-based catalyst is the power that children derive from their inaccurate conclusions founded in their magical thought, that promotes dysfunctional behavior. There are three types of power-based catalysts resulting from magical thoughts that children may experience:

1. Children active in destructive magical thought may believe that they have the power to be responsible for the loss.

   I got sick and I touched Grandpa and then he got sick and died.

   I heard them arguing about, me so it is my fault that my parents got divorced.

2. Children with magical thought may believe that they have the power to fix the loss.

   If I have the power to kill him, I have the power to bring him back to life.

   If I can get my parents in my counselor's office together, they will stay married.

3. Children with magical thought may believe that they can magically eliminate grief and the process of mourning for themselves and others.

   If I am perfectly good, my grief will go away.

These power-based catalysts, resulting from children's destructive magical thought, usually ignite dysfunctional behavior. Dysfunctional behavior is inconsistent with the tasks of healthy mourning.

THE MODEL OF MAGICAL THOUGHT– "SEEDS FOR THE DESTRUCTION OF CHILDREN'S PERSONALITY DEVELOPMENT"

It has been demonstrated through research that unresolved complicated mourning can effect the development of children's personality, creating potential personality disorders for some children as they become adults. Gorkin (1984) suggests that the failure of the mourning process leads to narcissistic personality disorder in some patients. Britchnell (1972) indicates with a longitudinal study that early bereavement affected females with three significant factors: personality disorders, depression, and alcoholism. Mallough, Abbey, and Gillies (1995) found a greater incidence of dependent personality disorder with patients who had an early loss. A model of how unresolved complicated mourning may adversely affect the development of children's personality is needed for practitioners to utilize for the treatment of complicated mourning for children.

When considering personality development and the process of mourning, there is one striking difference between children and adults. Most adults usually have their personalities developed while they are in a process of mourning. If adults do not have an actualized personality, then they may have a personality disorder. When children are mourning, their personalities are in the process of developing and their mourning (functional or dysfunctional) is incorporated within the development of their personalities (see Figure 1). Destructive magical

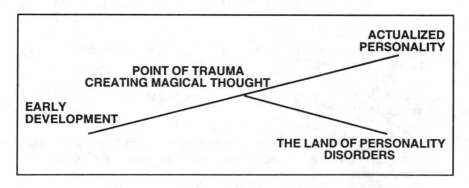

Figure 1. Personality development.

thought, related to mourning, may have the potential to damage the development of a child's personality. When trauma such as a loss with grief occurs, destructive magical thought may have the potential to draw children away from the development of their actualized personality, due to the development of defensive mechanisms and the creation of various personality disorders.

If bereaved children's destructive magical thought is never exposed or corrected, what effects might their magical thought have on children and their personality development? Consider the structure of the Model of Magical Thought offered below with an example of its effect on personality:

MAGICAL + COGNITIVE > DEFENSE > PERSONALITY
THOUGHTS DISTORTIONS MECHANISMS DISORDERS

KEY DEFINITIONS FOR THE MODEL
OF MAGICAL THOUGHT

Magical Thoughts

Magical thought is a child's inaccurate conclusion(s) regarding a loss experience resulting in the child believing that he or she is responsible for the loss experience and needs to fix the loss experience. Magical thought may lead a child to believe that he or she has developed a method of mourning, but the child has actually developed an unhealthy and complicated process of mourning.

Cognitive Distortions

Magical thought and cognitive distortions are two distinctly different concepts. For the purposes of this book and the Model of Magical Thought, cognitive distortions, such as the ten described in David Burns (1999) book "The Feeling Good Handbook," are restricting patterns of thought that fuel magical thought to develop into potential defense mechanisms and personality disorders. Magical thought offer children inaccurate conclusions, that are developed as children with incomplete cognitive equipment misinterpret their loss experiences. Children develop magical thought that they are responsible for a tragedy, convincing themselves that they can fix the tragic situation, and/or escape the tasks of healthy mourning. Cognitive distortions can attach to magical thought and fuel children into developing defense mechanisms and/or personality disorders. Cognitive distortion, such as black and white thinking, magnifying negatives and minimizing positives are common cognitive distortions children use to fuel their magical thoughts.

Personality

Abraham Maslow's (1987) theory of personality suggests that the development of a person to his or her full potential is founded on a hierarchy of needs including needs for safety, belongingness and love, esteem, and self-actualization. For this author, the development of children's personality to full potential can be disrupted by children's destructive magical thought founded on grief experiences. For example, children may be developing their personality in a healthy manner but, when a loss occurs, some children may develop magical thought which interferes with children's progression with their needs for safety, belongingness and love, esteem, and self-actualization.

Defense Mechanism

This author defines defense mechanism as a combination and pattern of thought and behavioral reactions that children exhibit, that reduce or eliminate the development of necessary skills required to develop self-actualized personalities. For example, when a teacher assertively confronts a boy, the boy has the choice to assert or he may choose to become passive-aggressive. If he is assertive, he will have an opportunity to further develop communication skills, interpersonal skills, and positive self-concept—all effecting personality development. If he chooses a passive-aggressive defense, he loses an opportunity to further develop communication skills, interpersonal skills, and positive self-concept, all effecting personality development.

Personality Disorder

This author defines personality disorder as persistent and rigid patterns of learned defense mechanisms that are out of control. Most of the personality disorders listed in DSM IV (1996) start with a defense; *dependent* personality disorder, *avoidant* personality disorder, *passive-aggressive* personality disorder, compulsive (*perfectionistic*) personality disorder, etc. As some children progress through childhood, adolescence, and into early adult life, they lose control of defense mechanisms replacing their actual personalities with rigid patterns of behavior reflecting personality disorders.

Magical thoughts fueled by cognitive distortions may develop into defense mechanisms and, for some children as they become adults, personality disorders. Consider the following example of Dora as she develops a personality disorder.

DORA

Dora was in therapy as an adult. Her history revealed that her father died when she was seven-years-old. After her father died, Dora regressed and became very clingy and dependent on her mother, which is not an unusual grief response. Many children develop a dependent response when mourning, but eventually let it go. However, Dora learned that there were benefits to being dependent. She learned that dependency offered her power and a feeling of safety. Dora realized that if she was dependent on others, people around her would do things for her and she could avoid dealing with the difficult realities of life. She replaced her developing ability to manage her own life with dependency upon others. If she had learned to manage her life, she would develop coping skills, communication skills, assertiveness, self-concept and gradually progress toward the development of an actualized personality. She was losing these skills because she started to rely on her MAGICAL THOUGHT that dependency gave her safety, so if she needed safety, she could attain safety by simply becoming dependent on others. It was easy for her to accept this one view without looking for other options because as a young child with concrete, linear reasoning, she concluded that if one option works, use it. Children with linear, concrete thinking do not have a natural tendency to look for multiple options. Her magical thought developed a power-based catalyst that helped Dora to believe, "I am too inadequate to handle life, so I need others to do it for me." Some bereaved children will eventually "let go" of this thought. Other children will continue within the Model of Magical Thought by fueling their magical thought with cognitive distortions. Her COGNITIVE DISTORTION of *all-or-none thinking* helped her conclude "The *only way* to have power and feel safe is by being dependent on others" fueling even further Dora's magical thought. By eliminating or not realizing all of the possible options to achieve safety, Dora locked herself into a pattern of dependency. Another COGNITIVE DISTORTION also fueling her magical thought of dependency was her *jumping to conclusions* about the future, "If I do it on my own, I will fail." Dora had convinced herself that it would be futile for her to attempt to be independent. Associated with Dora's magical thought and cognitive distortions was the secondary gain of avoiding the tension and stresses of managing her life as well as avoiding the tensions and stresses of developing an actualized personality. Dora's magical thought also had an expected wonderful outcome (a false outcome because it is founded on magical thought) advocating that she could always achieve safety by being dependent.

The combination of Dora's magical thought, fueled by cognitive distortions, eventually evolved into the development of DEFENSE MECHANISMS. Throughout Dora's childhood, when she became distressed or challenged, she would immediately choose to become dependent as a defensive reaction. Whomever she was dependent upon would come to her rescue and reduce the stresses in Dora's life. Dora's defense mechanism was *in her control* as she could choose when she would and would not utilize it. Each time she chose to use her defense mechanism of dependency, she lost opportunities to develop coping skills, communication skills, assertiveness skills, and self-concept, which inhibited progression toward her actualized personality. The word "avoidance" was becoming more significant in her life, as avoidance was an additional reinforcing secondary gain of her dependency. She focused so much time and energy into developing dependency, that she avoided processing healthy mourning. As Dora became an adolescent, her defense mechanisms eventually became all consuming and, instead of selectively using dependency as a defense mechanism, dependency became an uncontrollable pattern and was evident in all of her interactions. Dependency *was no longer in her control* and, as she progressed toward adulthood, she developed a comprehensive PERSONALITY DISORDER. Her *out of control* dependency personality disorder helped her to avoid the issues of life and also eliminated the development of her actualized personality.

Summary of Dora's Case

MAGICAL   + COGNITIVE > DEFENSES > PERSONALITY
THOUGHT   DISTORTIONS MECHANISMS   DISORDERS

Dora's personality disorder developed in accordance with the following magical thought structure:

Magical Thought
Power-Based Catalyst
"Dependency makes me feel safe, so to feel safe
all I have to do is be dependent."

Cognitive Distortion
Black and White Thinking
"The ONLY WAY to feel safe is by being dependent."

Defense Mechanisms
"When I am challenged, I will choose to become defensive
by becoming dependent."

Personality Disorder
"I will make a lifelong commitment to be dependent in
every situation and with everyone."

Dora's example demonstrates that the process of mourning, mis-guided by destructive magical thought, can eventually lead to severe personality disorders. Here are several other examples:

1. When Melissa was at the funeral home for her deceased father's visitation, she was told by her mother not to worry about father. Her mother attempted to reassure Melissa that it was not really her father in the casket, but a dummy with a look-alike mask. Her mother told Melissa that her father was on a secret mission and that he was not really dead. Melissa's mother was promoting an extreme and very dangerous magical thought with realistic consequences. As a young child, Melissa believed this tale and always wondered why her father would not come to visit her. Eventually, she learned of her father's death when she overheard a family discussion about him. She became enraged with unexpressed anger toward her mother. Melissa learned a very important and destructive lesson from this distorted death story. She accepted the belief that she could not handle life and its emotions, because her mother had hidden the real issues of life with fanciful tales. This inaccurate conclusion became a power-based catalyst, which was at the core of her destructive magical thought. Since Melissa was a young child without abstract thinking, she did not conclude that her mother had lied due to her mother's inadequacies. When she heard the truth from another source, she understood that her mother had lied to her, but Melissa assumed her mother lied because Melissa was incapable of handling the truth. In other words, Melissa assumed she was lied to, not because her mother could not effectively deal with reality, but because Melissa was incapable of dealing with reality. For Melissa to realize that this lie was her mother's issue would require abstract reasoning, which had not yet developed in Melissa. Melissa began to develop in accordance with the Model of Magical Thought.

Magical Thought
Power-Based Catalyst
"I cannot handle the realities of life, so I need to deny
the existence of the painful realities of life"

<u>Cognitive Distortion</u>
Black and White Thinking
"The ONLY WAY to handle the painful realities of life
is by denying their existence."

<u>Defense Mechanism</u>
"When I have to handle a painful reality of life, I can
CHOOSE to deny its existence."

<u>Personality Disorder</u>
"My denial is OUT OF CONTROL and I deny the existence
of all painful realities of life."

Melissa's destructive magical thoughts are now arranged for a very co-dependent lifestyle with the denial of all of life's problems. Melissa's personality developed with the belief that in order to have a relationship with her mother, and eventually others, she would have to accept their belief systems and deny her own conclusions about reality. The impact of her magical thought extended past her youth. For example, as an adult when she married an alcoholic, she believed that her husband was not an alcoholic no matter what turmoil she experienced from living with him. An entire lifestyle of denial developed for Melissa, founded on a powerful grief-related magical thought promoted by her mother.

2. Often children create destructive magical thoughts on their own even when parents do everything right. Consider this example of perfectionism. An eighteen-year-old female named Brenda, who had an above average IQ of 120, was admitted in a psychiatric hospital after she had made a very serious suicide attempt. She had recently graduated third in her class from a very large high school—an extraordinary event considering that her IQ suggests an astute intellect, but not a gifted classification. She tried to commit suicide because she was not first in her class. Even though she was in a very large graduating class, she could not enjoy her third place ranking. When a complete socio-emotional history was taken within initial therapy sessions, it became apparent that Brenda had a destructive magical thought related to a loss experience. When she was a concrete-thinking elementary school child, her older brother died. When she and her family were mourning she noticed that when she acted perfect that her parents appeared to feel better, and this made her feel better. Her parents were caring people who did not have knowledge about the process of mourning, as many people in this culture do not. When Brenda's brother died, her parents felt encouraged because they could see Brenda was

functioning better since the death of her brother and they believed she was making a good adjustment. Brenda, like a large segment of children who are developing a complicated process of mourning, actually appeared to be making a good adjustment as her grades were better, she did chores she never did before, and she seemed to have a good attitude. None of her normal grief emotions were ever expressed, which meant that her normal and healing grief emotions were not active and therefore not serving their combined purpose of processing healthy mourning. Underneath her glowing exterior Brenda buried her normal grief emotions with destructive magical thought:

<u>Magical Thought</u>
Power-Based Catalyst
"When I am perfect, my parents feel better and I feel better
so all I have to do is be perfect."

<u>Cognitive Distortion</u>
Black and White Thinking
"The ONLY WAY to feel better is by being compulsively
perfectionistic."

<u>Defense Mechanism</u>
"When I am stressed by others or life, I will CHOOSE to
be compulsively perfectionistic."

<u>Personality Disorder</u>
"I am now OUT OF CONTROL with compulsive
perfectionism."

Brenda had lost her actualized personality due to a destructive magical thought related to the death of her brother. An important factor, when considering the Model of Magical Thought for children, is that their magical thought is developing as their personalities are developing. This factor makes children susceptible to powerful and possibly life-changing damage—the loss of personality by developing personality disorders ignited by magical thought and fueled by cognitive distortions.

3. Anger offers children the illusion of power. Children who are mourning often feel a definite lack of empowerment. They cannot bring their dead loved one back to life. They cannot make their parents stay married. They cannot make their grief reactions disappear. Children may choose to fixate on anger because it offers them a facade of power. Anger offers momentary power, but it is quite destructive in its long-term effects. Children with concrete thinking or even immature

abstract reasoning, may not realize the long-term destructive effects of anger and they may indulge in the immediate gratifying effects of anger. The sixteen-year-old boy previously discussed in Chapter 2 in the section "Adolescence—Abstract Thought Unleashed" whose parents were divorcing, became very angry with his father and pushed his father's buttons. This sixteen-year-old boy felt very unempowered due to his inability to stop his parents' divorce. When he pushed his father's buttons he felt empowerment due to his father's intense reaction, which was quite enticing since this boy felt little empowerment to effect any other change. This created a power-based catalyst that attached magical thought to his personality development, diverting him from the tasks of healthy mourning.

<u>Magical Thought</u>
Power-Based Catalyst
"Anger gives me power."

<u>Cognitive Distortion</u>
Black and White Thinking
"The ONLY WAY to have power is by being angry."

Labeling
"If I label adults as 'authority figures', I have many places
to release and DISPLACE my anger on others."

<u>Defense Mechanism</u>
"When I want to feel powerful, I can CHOOSE to use anger
by being passive-aggressive and/or antisocial."

<u>Personality Disorder</u>
"I am now OUT OF CONTROL with passive-aggressive
and/or antisocial reactions."

Angry children adhering to the Model of Magical Thought can lose their actualized personality by developing angry passive-aggressive reactions and/or angry antisocial reactions, leading to defense mechanisms and possibly the development of personality disorder(s). With the development of anti-social personality disorder, as children with grief-related anger develop, they lose the original target of their anger because they rely too heavily on displacing their anger on others. For example, if an angry teenager labels most adults as "authority figures" then the teenager has many people to displace anger, effectively avoiding his or her loss experience and associated mourning. Often angry teenagers over rely on the cognitive distortion of labeling others as authority figures, which allows them many avenues to displace their anger. Displacement can provide fuel for the development of anti-social personality disorders. Displacement allows bereaved children to lose the targets of their original anger (the loss experience), which can result in complicated mourning. Instead of concentrating on the tasks of healthy mourning, angry teenagers tend to continue to displace anger, eventually ruining their own reputations and relationships.

4. When previously discussing anguish in Chapter 1, a description was offered of an anguished eight-year-old boy whose parents gave him "everything" and he isolated in his bedroom. This boy was excessively isolating himself without positive interaction with family and friends. His parents had great intentions when they were buying him all of those material objects. They could see that he was harboring feelings of horrendous anguish due to his brother's death. His parents did not realize that anguish was a necessary part of his process of mourning and his parents felt a strong protective desire to take away his painful anguish. His parents discovered that when they bought him a new toy, he appeared distracted from his anguish and he seemed happy. Their desire to eliminate his anguish became stronger than the realization that this cycle of distraction could eventually spin out of control with destructive magical thought. His parents continued to buy him out of his anguish, which resulted in the enhancement of this boy's destructive magical thoughts. Obtaining objects became a compulsion for him with shorter periods of resolution occurring after each purchase. He concluded that his parents felt that he could never cope with his loss and that distraction was a better route. Distraction on material objects replaced his embracing of his process of mourning and bonding with others.

Magical Thought
Power-Based Catalyst
"I can cope with grief by distracting myself with objects
so I will never have to mourn."

Cognitive Distortion
Black and White Thinking
"The ONLY WAY to cope with grief is with
distraction on objects."

Defense Mechanism
"I will CHOOSE to distract myself from grief by putting
pressure on my parents to buy me stuff."

<u>Personality Disorder</u>
"I will compulsively (OUT OF CONTROL) buy things to
distract myself from my grief."

The suppression of children's normal grief emotions, in this case anguish, may account for the development of many compulsions such as indulgence of food, materialism, perfectionism, rigidity, spending, stubbornness, religiosity, excessive visual stimulation (television, video games, Internet, etc.), and much more. Anguish is an emotional void that needs filling. As a result of too much indulgence and this eight-year-old boy's inaccurate interpretations, he developed in accordance with the Model of Magical Thought.

Each of these children accepted powerful and destructive magical thought that distorted their perceptions of themselves and their ability to advance through their process of mourning. Their destructive magical thought offered a strong power-based catalyst, additionally fueled by cognitive distortions. These children also received "secondary gains," which reinforced their continued progression in accordance with the Model of Magical Thought.

EXAMPLES OF THE POWER OF
SECONDARY GAINS

Listed below are examples of the secondary gains from the cases mentioned in this chapter:

- If Dora is dependent on others, she never has to manage the complexities of life.
- If Melissa can deny the existence of all problems, she can stay within a comfortable zone of safety, never taking the risk to develop her own belief system, positive self-concept, and personality.
- Perfectionistic Brenda will not have to feel the painful emotions of grief, if she focuses only on maintaining perfectionism to make herself and her parents feel better.
- An angry adolescent, who displaces his anger on others, never has to focus on himself and face the painful emotions and reality that accompany his loss.
- Through isolation the eight-year-old boy can distract himself by focusing on buying material objects (an external focus) and never embrace the uncomfortable but necessary tasks of healthy mourning.

Destructive, power-based magical thought guides children toward the development of defensiveness and, for some children, personality disorder, while secondary gains continually demonstrate to children the advantages of advancing in accordance with the destructive Model of Magical Thought.

PARENT SUGGESTION

Parents should not attempt to diagnose their children based on this Model of Magical Thought. Parents can serve the useful purpose of supplying information and insights to grief therapists who are trained in assisting children with complicated mourning. Parents can have a listening ear for their children's magical thoughts. Parents can also observe children's behavior, which often offers telltale links to the existence of magical thought. These parental functions provide valuable information for parents to offer grief therapists.

SUMMARY

The Model of Magical Thought is founded on inaccurate conclusions children develop as they misinterpret their loss experiences, resulting in power-based catalysts including:

1. Children active in destructive magical thought believe that they have the power to be responsible for the loss.
2. Children with magical thought believe that they have the power to fix the loss.
3. Children with magical thought may believe that they have the power to magically eliminate the process of mourning.

The Model of Magical Thought has a structure describing the development of defense mechanisms and personality disorders founded on magical thought related to grief issues. Inaccurate conclusions, children develop about their responsibility for the death and/or how to process their mourning, inhibits children's progression with the tasks of healthy mourning. Children's inaccurate conclusions may be fueled with cognitive distortions creating defense mechanisms and, for some children as they develop into adults, personality disorders.

The two-part goal of parents and grief therapists, when assisting children with complicated mourning founded on magical thought, is to eliminate destructive magical thought and to help children rehearse adaptive behavior reflecting the tasks of healthy mourning.

CHAPTER 4

The Tasks of Healthy Mourning Distorted by Destructive Magical Thought

The tasks of healthy mourning can be used as guideposts to assist in determining if children are processing mourning in a healthy manner. If children are progressing with healthy mourning, they do not harbor significant and constant destructive magical thought. If children are not progressing with healthy mourning, destructive magical thoughts may exist. The Model of Magical Thought can be utilized with any author's tasks of healthy mourning. To demonstrate the utility of the Model of Magical Thought, I have chosen four tasks from William Worden, Ph.D. (1982, 1991) and one task from Alan Wolfelt, Ph.D. (1988). Tasks from Therese Rando, Ph.D. (1993) will also be listed with discussion for those who prefer to utilize her tasks.

READER NOTE

When I am referring to Task I, Task II, Task III, Task IV, and Task V throughout this book, I am referring to the tasks listed below. William Worden wrote the first four tasks and Alan Wolfelt wrote the fifth task. To make the tasks clinically applicable, this author has offered additional thoughts for several of the tasks.

THE FIVE TASKS OF HEALTHY MOURNING

The four tasks of mourning from William Worden (1982, 1991) are listed below:

Task I: To accept the reality of the loss.

William Worden (1991) expresses this task well when he stated "Part of the acceptance of reality is to come to the belief that reunion is impossible, at least in this life" (p. 11).

Task II: To work through to the pain of grief.

William Worden (1991) indicates that it is necessary to work through to the pain of grief to avoid "symptoms or other form of aberrant behavior." I define the pain of grief as the normal emotions of grief, described in Chapter 2 of this book, which have the shared purpose of helping children to maintain their process of healthy mourning.

Task III: To adjust to the environment in which the deceased is missing.

One of my favorite questions for children which reflects this task is, "Since you have had these losses, what do you do to make yourself feel better?" In other words, how are you adjusting to your environment?

Task IV: To withdraw emotional energy and reinvest it in another relationship.

In clinical practice I utilize Dr. Worden's (1982) older definition of this task which focused on developing new healthy relationships after the death of a loved one. To progress with this task, children need to develop healthy relationships that do not involve "people replacement." People replacement is defined as children's attempts to force others to be exactly like the loved one who died.

An additional task of grief from Alan Wolfelt (1988):

Task V: To convert the relationship with the deceased from one of presence to a relationship of memory.

In clinical practice it is helpful to separate the tasks of developing new relationships from establishing a relationship with the memory of the dead loved one. In clinical practice, clients tend to become confused when both tasks are offered together as they are in Dr. Worden's (1991) second edition of "Grief Counseling & Grief Therapy." For the purposes of this book Dr. Worden's (1982) Task IV focuses on developing new relationships and Dr. Wolfelt's (1988) task focuses on establishing a relationship with the memory of the dead loved one. I would add that it is important to establish a relationship with the "accurate" memory of the dead loved one. Children should not glorify the positive aspects of the dead loved one, editing the negative aspects. Nor should children only focus on the negative aspects of the dead loved one, editing the positive aspects. Some children, raised with parents engaged with chemical dependency and abuse, may glorify the favorite vice of the dead parent. Instead of focusing on the abusive aspects of an alcoholic parent who died, children may only focus on the colorful stories associated with their parents' vice, while editing the abusive effects of their parents' chemical dependency.

Example of a colorful story associated with a parent's vice:

> I remember when Dad was so drunk, he came home and beat up the Christmas tree.

Anytime children edit truth and reality (including the editing of accurate memories), there is a greater potential they will damage their processing of the tasks of healthy mourning.

Children who are mourning have two choices. They can either progress with the tasks of healthy mourning without magical thought which results in a healthy mourning, or children can progress in accordance with the Model of Magical Thought which inhibits/stops/redirects their process of healthy mourning, converting it into a complicated mourning. Consider this author's unhealthy examples (with magical thought) and healthy examples (without magical thought) of each of William Worden's (1982) four tasks of mourning as well as Alan Wolfelt's (1988) task, regarding establishing a memory of the dead loved one.

TASK I: TO ACCEPT THE REALITY OF THE LOSS

Unhealthy example WITH Magical Thought:

A woman's husband was killed in a car accident leaving her to survive with their three young children. For many months after his death, they always waited every evening for him to come home. After several years their "waiting" persisted, as each evening they waited to hear the familiar noises of him returning. They were stuck in a process of complicated mourning. The family shared the magical thought that if they expected him to return, he would return. At a cognitive level they all knew he was dead and buried, but they still waited for him to come home. Their magical thought of "if they expected him, he would return" was inhibiting their ability to accept the reality of his death.

This shared magical thought was stopping this family from progressing through Task I.

Healthy example WITHOUT Magical Thought:

A little five-year-old girl did everything she could to stop her parents from divorcing. She held the belief that if she could get her parents in her therapist's office that her therapist would magically make her parents stay together. She engaged in every behavior possible to get them in the therapy office. Finally, she realized that her parents would never get back together and she quit trying to get them in the therapy office. She relinquished her belief and it did not become ingrained within the Model of Magical Thought. She did not fuel magical thought with cognitive distortions, so she did not develop defense mechanisms and personality disorders. She was accepting the reality that the divorce was going to occur, which resulted in progression through Task I.

TASK II: TO WORK THROUGH TO THE PAIN OF GRIEF

Unhealthy examples WITH Magical Thought:

An excellent example of an unhealthy digression from Task II is the boy who was given toys whenever he felt anguish. This boy concluded, "I can distract myself from the pain of grief by focusing on objects." His magical thought stopped him from working through the normal emotional pain of grief.

Another unhealthy example of not progressing through Task II would be a child who has the magical thought, "If I talk about my grief emotions, it will make my mother upset and cry. If I keep my grief emotions to myself, she will not become upset." This child believes that he or she has the power to protect mother from the pain of grief by inhibiting the expression of his grief emotions, which inhibits progression through Task II.

Healthy example WITHOUT Magical Thought:

A girl feels anguish and expresses her anguish to her mother who also feels anguish. As they talk about their anguish together they bond, creating safe ground to talk about their emotions and pain of grief. Because this girl has not progressed in accordance with the Model of Magical Thought, she could freely discuss her grief emotions without fear of hurting others, which results in bonding with her important adults who are also mourning. This girl is progressing through Task II, as she is working through the emotional pain of grief.

TASK III: TO ADJUST TO THE ENVIRONMENT IN WHICH THE DECEASED IS MISSING

Unhealthy example WITH Magical Thought:

A second-grade boy, who is mourning the recent death of his father, feared having emotional reactions in the classroom. Prior to his father's death, he was often teased by several of the children in his classroom. He anticipated that if he became emotional about his father's death at school, these children would pounce on the opportunity to tease him. One day on the playground he became emotional and he was teased. Through his frustration he became violent, harboring the magical thought that violence was the only way he could respond and control the teasing of others in his school environment. His inability to perceive options (concrete thinking) coupled with the magical thought that violence was his only solution, stopped him from adjusting to his school environment. He did not progress in this task of mourning, due to a magical thought reflecting violence.

Healthy example WITHOUT Magical Thought:

This same boy was offered a safe spot—a private place where he could choose to go to experience his grief emotions. This safe spot offered him empowerment, as he had the choice to have his grief reaction in the classroom or he could go to his safe spot to experience grief emotions. When he was with children he trusted, he could choose to have his emotional reactions with those children. When he was with children with whom he did not feel safe, he could choose to go to his safe spot. His safe spot offered him an option that allowed him to adjust to his school environment. The development of a safe spot helped this child progress through this task of mourning, without the development of destructive magical thought.

TASK IV: TO WITHDRAW EMOTIONAL ENERGY AND REINVEST IT IN ANOTHER RELATIONSHIP

Unhealthy example WITH Magical Thought:

A young girl's favorite aunt dies. She starts to establish a relationship with another aunt. Eventually she puts pressure on this aunt to be exactly like the deceased aunt. She wants this aunt to be interested in all the same activities as the deceased aunt. She wants this aunt to act and say the things that made the deceased aunt unique. This girl is attempting to "people replace." She has the magical belief that she can get her dead aunt back, by forcing her surviving aunt to be just like the deceased aunt. She is not developing a new healthy relationship with her surviving aunt if she is attempting to use her surviving aunt to replace her dead aunt. She is investing in a relationship with a dead person and not establishing a new relationship, which is counter to this task of mourning. A magical thought is stopping her from progressing through this task.

Healthy example WITHOUT Magical Thought:

A girl's favorite aunt dies. Even though she still loves the deceased aunt, she starts to establish a relationship with another aunt. Instead of putting pressure on the surviving aunt to be just like the deceased aunt, she develops a relationship with the surviving aunt based on their mutual interests. She develops this relationship with her surviving aunt without the pressure of forcing that aunt to be exactly like the deceased aunt. She is progressing through this task of mourning, as she is investing in a new relationship.

TASK V: TO CONVERT THE RELATIONSHIP WITH THE DECEASED FROM ONE OF PRESENCE TO A RELATIONSHIP OF MEMORY

Unhealthy example WITH Magical Thought:

A girl's father has died. She creates a shrine for her father. She attempts to isolate herself so she can interact with her father's shrine. When she is interacting with her father's possessions in the shrine, she pretends he is still alive focusing on the glorified memories of her father. She is so focused on the glorified memories of her father, she edits the reality of his alcoholism and physical abusiveness. She has established a relationship with the incomplete memory of her father based on the magical thought, "I can have the fantasy parent I always wanted, by only remembering the few positive memories of my father." She is not progressing through this task of mourning, due to a magical thought that edits painful but important memories of her father. She is editing reality, which allows room for the development of magical thought.

Healthy example WITHOUT Magical Thought:

The entire family creates a "memory table" and all family members put a special item on the table that they recall was associated with the person who died. Later they gathered together to recall the deceased person and they remember all of the person's neat qualities as well as defenses and points of irritation. They are remembering the unedited and complete person, instead of editing out reality and fostering the development of destructive magical thought. They are progressing through this task of mourning by remembering every aspect of their deceased loved one.

TYING IT ALL TOGETHER

This next paragraph, which includes another definition of complicated mourning, is *THE MOST IMPORTANT PARAGRAPH* in this book:

> If a child is not progressing through one task of mourning, a combination of tasks of mourning, or all the tasks of mourning, it is quite likely that a destructive magical thought exists, creating a complicated mourning. If a child is not progressing through the healthy tasks of mourning, he or she may be in accordance with the Model of Magical Thought, developing a power-based catalyst, fueled with cognitive distortions, and creating potential defense mechanisms and/or personality disorders. When there is a lack of progress in children's healthy and healing process of mourning, the caregiver should look for the existence of magical thoughts.

Several writers have offered types of complicated mourning that may demonstrate magical thought more prominently.

COMPLICATED MOURNING

Various phrases have been offered to describe processes that suggest unhealthy mourning including complicated mourning, disenfranchised grief, dysfunctional mourning, and more. Below is a listing of the various avenues where mourning can go awry and become complicated, as described by Alan Wolfelt (1991), Therese Rando (1993), and Kenneth Doka (1989). As this author reads the various descriptions of complicated mourning, this author finds that, for many children, the basis of each could be grounded in destructive magical thought.

Alan Wolfelt (1991) has offered the following typology of complicated mourning.

Absent Grief

Alan Wolfelt (1991) defines absent grief as "In absent grief no apparent feelings of grief are expressed" (p. 30).

Absent Grief Explained with the Model of Magical Thought

In initial mourning, it is not uncommon for children to feel numb and stunned, a normal but temporary grief reaction that inhibits normal grief emotions. Some children may place destructive magical thoughts on "not feeling grief emotions" that manifest into intense blocking, well beyond their temporary numb and stunned reactions. For example, the perfectionistic child may develop the magical thought, "When I am perfect, I feel better so to feel better all I have to do is be perfect." Instead of progressing through Task II and feeling the normal grief emotions, this child focuses on the constant pursuit of perfectionism. This perfectionistic child offers the appearance of making a good adjustment after the death of a loved one, but never demonstrates normal grief emotions such as commotion, attempts to re-create, anguish, sadness, and others. Another child may harbor the magical thought, "When I show my grief emotions, it hurts my mother and makes her feel bad. I will not show emotions, which will help my mother feel better." This child has wonderful intentions, but has developed a power-based catalyst in accordance with the Model of Magical Thought allowing him or her to believe that he or she can control mother's emotional state. With this magical thought the child has not only stopped expressing normal grief emotions (Task II), but the child has also eliminated the possibility of bonding with mother, which is counter to Task IV—investing in other relationships.

Distorted Grief

Alan Wolfelt (1989) defines a distorted grief as, "a distortion occurs in one or more of the normal dimensions of grief. This distortion may prevent the grief process from unfolding and the person often becomes fixated on the distorted dimension of the grief" (p. 30).

Distorted Grief Explained with the Model of Magical Thought

One example of distorted grief is the child who accepts the magical thought, "Power can only be attained by utilizing anger." Anger becomes so effective in keeping normal grief emotions at bay that a child relies on anger alone, in accordance with the Model of Magical Thought, evolving an anger-based defense mechanism and possibly an anger-based personality disorder (passive-aggressive personality disorder and/or antisocial personality disorder).

A girl may only demonstrate "attempts to re-create" based on her longing for the dead loved one but never feeling the other normal grief emotions. In her attempts to re-create, she forces people to be just like the person who died, fostering her magical thought, "I can get the dead loved one back by finding a replacement." She practices the Model of Magical Thought by focusing so intensely on getting the dead loved one back, so her other normal grief emotions are never experienced or expressed. If other normal grief emotions surface she pursues her attempts to get the dead loved one back more fervently to push other grief emotions away, maintaining her magical thought.

Converted Grief

Alan Wolfelt (1991) defines converted grief as "the person demonstrates behaviors and symptoms, which result in personal distress; however, he or she is unable to relate their presence to the loss" (p. 30).

Converted Grief Explained with the Model of Magical Thought

An example of converted grief is a fourteen-year-old male teenager who is angry because his parents were divorced, but he does not realize their divorce is the reason he is angry. He is mourning the death of his parents' marriage but he is too busy displacing his anger onto others, which results in losing his original understanding—he is angry due to his parents' divorce. His magical thought may suggest, "If I am busy displacing anger on others, I do not have to acknowledge the actual loss and the emotions I feel about their divorce." If he focuses on displacing anger, he never feels the connection with his anger and loss experience.

Another boy may feel the normal grief emotion of anguish, but learns to believe that experiencing anguish is abnormal. His parents may give him a new toy to make him feel happy whenever he experiences anguish. He develops converted grief because, instead of realizing anguish is a part of health mourning, he believes that when he feels anguish it is because he is abnormal. His conclusion becomes a power-based catalyst that nudges him into accordance with the Model of Magical Thought, "To be normal I must design ways to not realize the impact of the divorce and to not feel the associated anguish." Displacement is a defensive mechanism which children often use to detach from their normal grief emotions from their loss experiences. "If I stay angry at everyone, I do not have to focus on the feelings I have about my loss experience."

Chronic Grief

Alan Wolfelt (1991) defines chronic grief as "the person demonstrates a persistent pattern of intense grief that does not result in appropriate reconciliation. The continued foci are the person who died, over valuing objects that belonged to the deceased, and depressive brooding. Essentially the mourner attempts to keep the person alive" (p. 30).

Chronic Grief Explained with the Model of Magical Thought

Often children who are ruminating with the dead loved one's objects are pretending the dead loved one is alive, which is a magical thought and counter to the tasks of healthy mourning. One possible magical thought a child may use is, "If I pretend my dead loved one is alive by focusing on his objects, he is alive." Another mourning child may continually try to "people replace" by forcing others to be exactly like the dead person. This child keeps the dead person alive and attempts to engage with the dead person via a replacement, harboring the magical thought, "I can get my dead loved one back by replacing him, if I can force others to be exactly like him." Both examples demonstrate children who are falling in accordance with the Model of Magical Thought.

It is easy to see that various magical thought processes may motivate each of these types of complicated mourning. Children, who are experiencing complicated mourning, are driven by power-based magical thought fueled by cognitive distortions and reinforced by the secondary gains. Children can develop the complicated mourning processes described above, founded on magical thought.

THERESE RANDO'S SIX "R" RESPONSE[1]

Therese Rando (1993) has offered an excellent categorization regarding complicated mourning. Listed are categories Therese Rando (1993) has developed, each with several complicated processes of mourning, which she has defined. Consider what potential magical thoughts children may develop regarding Therese Rando's (1993) various definitions of complicated mourning. The six "R" Processes listed are Therese Rando's (1993) tasks of healthy mourning. The

[1] From *Treatment of Complicated Mourning* (p. 156) by T. A. Rando, 1993, Champaign, IL: Research Press. Copyright 1993 by T. A. Rando. Reprinted by permission.

narrative with each "R" Process is my explanation of the Model of Magical Thought with Therese Rando's (1993) typology of complicated mourning:

Type of Complicated Mourning	Definition	Location of Initial Interference of the R Process
Absent Mourning	". . . it is as if the death has not occurred at all."	Recognize the loss (first "R" process)

Absent mourning may result from children completely denying the death occurred, suppressing the normal grief emotions, or feeling the normal grief but not expressing it. Consider these possible magical thoughts that could initiate these three types of absent mourning.

Three examples of magical thought associated with absent mourning:

1. Denying the Death Occurred

If my loved one did not die, I do not have to mourn his death.

2. Suppressing the Normal Grief Emotions

If I am perfect, I will feel better.

3. Feeling the Normal Grief Emotions but not Expressing Them:

If I do not show my emotions, I am strong.

Type of Complicated Mourning	Definition	Location of Initial Interference of the R Process
Delayed Mourning	"In delayed mourning syndrome, a full or partial mourning reaction is eventually triggered, bringing the period of delay or relative delay to an end."	React to the separation (second "R" process)

Scarlet O'Hara in *Gone with the Wind,* made delayed mourning famous. When faced with a trauma, including her mother's death, she would instruct herself by saying, "I won't think about that now, I'll just think about that tomorrow." Although there are times when it is necessary to delay mourning, magical thought may permeate the decision to delay mourning.

An example of magical thought associated with delayed mourning:

I will lose control of myself if I feel my grief emotions, so to maintain control of myself I will not feel grief emotions now.

Type of Complicated Mourning	Definition	Location of Initial Interference of the R Process
Inhibited Mourning	". . . in complicated mourning through inhibition the (mourning) process consciously and/or unconsciously becomes and remains restricted to various degrees."	React to the separation Recollect and re-experience the deceased and the relationship (second and third "R" processes)

Dr. Rando (1993) uses the example, "a bereaved individual might refrain from review of the deceased and the lost relationship to avoid confrontation with aspects of that person and relationship previously eliciting anger" (pp. 162-163). A bereaved individual's tendency to avoid confrontation by utilizing anger may have been fostered by a magical thought.

An example of magical thought associated with inhibited mourning:

If I inhibit the memory of the loved one, I do not have to confront the memory of his anger.

Type of Complicated Mourning	Definition	Location of Initial Interference of the R Process
Distorted Mourning	Extreme anger or extreme guilt.	React to the separation Recollect and re-experience the deceased and the relationship (second and third "R" processes)

Distorted mourning is the presence of extreme anger or extreme guilt to the exclusion of other grief emotions. One of the reasons why some children develop a distorted mourning, founded on anger, is to avoid the pain created by their grief emotions.

An example of magical thought associated with distorted mourning:

If I am busy angrily blaming others, then I do not have to attend to and feel my grief emotions.

Type of Complicated Mourning	Definition	Location of Initial Interference of the R Process
Conflicted Mourning	". . . arises after a loss of highly troubled and con-	React to the separation Recollect and

flicted relationships. After brief absence of grief—even relief—the mourner experiences severe guilt, self-reproach . . . as well as the same mixed feelings that had characterized the premorbid relationship." re-experience the deceased and the relationship (second and third "R" processes)

Therese Rando (1993) refers to the definition of conflicted mourning offered by Parkes and Weiss (1983) that refers to mourning that is founded on a loss of a "highly troubled, ambivalent relationships." This author has counseled many children who were mourning the death of an abusive parent. Children in the process of a conflicted mourning often have two emotions that they believe are in opposition and create confusion for children. Children who have had an abusive parent who has died will often feel relief and anguish. Children do not understand that they can experience two emotional states at one time. Children do not realize that these two emotional states (relief and anguish) are founded on two different issues. Children may feel relief that they are no longer being abused and they can also feel anguish that they will never have the fantasy parent that they always wanted.

An example of magical thought associated with conflicted mourning:

> If I have two conflicting emotions about an abusive parent who died, I am not normal. I need to get rid of one of these emotional states.

Type of Complicated Mourning	Definition	Location of Initial Interference of the R Process
Unanticipated Mourning	Unexpected death or terminal illness including the main complicated issues associated with unanticipated loss.	Recognize the loss (first "R" process)

Often associated with unanticipated mourning is guilt and/or a tendency to scapegoat, which can produce magical thought within children.

An example of magical thought associated with unanticipated mourning:

> I asked my Dad to go to the store to buy me a toy and on the way to the store he died in a car accident. It is my fault that he died. I will never ask people to do things for me ever again.

Type of Complicated Mourning	Definition	Location of Initial Interference of the R Process
Chronic Mourning	". . . acute mourning that persists interminably— that fails to draw to its natural conclusion and in which intense reaction do not abate over time."	Relinquish the old attach- ments to the deceased and the old assumptive world. Readjust to move adap- tively into the new world without forgetting the old (fourth and fifth "R" processes).

Children may have struggles relinquishing the attachments to the deceased and the old assumptive world and not make healthy adjustments to a new world without their loved one. "People replacement" is a dysfunctional process that involves children attempting to force surviving loved ones to be exactly like the dead loved one. When "people replacement" occurs children become stuck in a pattern of attempting to continue to have a relationship with their dead loved one. When this pattern occurs, children never relinquish themselves from their dead loved one and the old assumptive world and they do not adapt to the new world without the dead loved one.

One example of magical thought associated with chronic mourning:

> If I can force others to be just like my dead loved one, I will not have to adjust to a world without my dead loved one.

DISENFRANCHISED GRIEF

Kenneth Doka, Ph.D. (1989), with his thorough study of disenfranchised grief, has categorized three main types of disenfranchised grief with a global definition:

Global Definition of Disenfranchised Grief

> . . . the grief that persons experience when they incur a loss that is not or cannot be openly acknowledged, publicly mourned, or socially supported (p. 4).

Three Types of Disenfranchised Grief

1. The relationship is not recognized. Examples include non-kin relationships such as "lovers, friends, neighbors, foster parents, colleagues, in-laws, stepparents and stepchildren, caregivers, counselors,

co-workers, and roommates (for example, in nursing homes). . . ."
Relationships that are not socially sanctioned, including "extramarital affairs, cohabitation, and homosexual relationships. . . ."

I purport that magical thought can develop and be shared by cultures, communities, and families. This type of disenfranchised grief suggests the possibility that a magical thought has been developed and shared by this culture, suggesting "Grief is only intense if you are mourning the death of a family member. So you should not have intense grief reactions for losses of non-kin." This culturally-based magical thought is contrary to the reality that some people are more emotionally bonded to non-kin relationships. This culturally-based magical thought offers a power-based catalyst advocating a conclusion that if a bereaved person has intense mourning for a non-kin relationship, something is wrong with the bereaved person.

2. The loss is not recognized, as the loss in not defined by society as significant. Kenneth Doka (1989) cites examples, which include abortion, pet loss, and psychological death (resulting from coma).

A culture that offers a lack of education can promote magical thought. If a culture does not educate its members about death and grief, magical thought can flourish. A common example of this type of disenfranchised grief is quick "pet replacement" for children when their pet dies. Instead of allowing and educating children to progress through the tasks of healthy mourning when a pet dies, parents of this culture will often immediately buy another pet suggesting the magical thought, "You can avoid mourning if you replace your loved one." This culturally-based magical thought instructs children that when a pet dies, quick replacement is a better solution than progressing with the tasks of healthy mourning.

3. The griever is not recognized. A person may be socially defined as not able to grieve. Dr. Doka (1989) offers examples, such as the very young, the elderly, the mentally disturbed, and the mentally retarded.

Our culture's magical thought may suggest, "Since he is mentally retarded, he is not able to mourn." People with mental retardation have the intellectual capacity of a person of several months of age to eight years of age. The discussion on cognition in Chapter 2 of this book suggests that people having this range of mental capacity does allow them an ability to mourn. Adults with mental retardation may mourn in a comparable fashion to children with concrete thinking skills.

The various types of disenfranchised grief that Dr. Doka (1989) defines may reflect destructive magical thought that is culturally and/or socially developed and advocated and poses great potential in inhibiting the tasks of healthy mourning.

Consider the following magical thoughts from the American culture that stop the bereaved from being recognized:

"If I get revenge, my grief will be resolved."
This magical thought is the quick-fix theme of many Hollywood movies.
"Big boys do not cry."
With this magical thought males are not easily recognized as mourners because normal grief emotions are inhibited.
"You will have to be the little dad/mom in the family."
This magical thought suggests that if children take on a new role, they will not need to mourn.
"Just get it (grief) behind you."
This simple magical thought advocates that children utilize denial.
"Everything happens for the best."
This common cultural magical thought attempts to erase a need for the normal grief emotions.

Children in this culture are developing with common cultural expressions filled with magical thought that assist in inhibiting/disrupting/eliminating the process of healthy mourning. This cultural tendency, the new and perplexing grief emotions, and children's developing but incomplete cognition, all contribute to children and their personal development of magical thought that thwarts their ability to process healthy mourning.

UTILIZING THE MODEL OF MAGICAL THOUGHT WITH THE TASKS OF MOURNING

Identifying the Clinical Issue

The concept of the Model of Magical Thought, with the guideposts of the tasks of healthy mourning, can be utilized to determine if children's process of mourning is healthy or misdirected by destructive magical thought, diverting the process of mourning onto an unhealthy path. The Model of Magical Thought can also assist in defining the clinical issue which is the destructive magical thought that begins the progression toward the development of defense mechanisms and potential personality disorders.

Study the following examples, which demonstrate how grief issues may be utilized in a healthy manner or may be adversely effected by the existence of destructive magical thought:

EXAMPLE 1

A grief consultant is advising a grief therapist. The grief therapist is counseling a family that consists of a mother, father, and three siblings. A fourth child died of leukemia five years ago. The grief therapist is concerned because during visits to the family home, she noticed that the dead child's bedroom was unchanged. This bedroom, although clean and fresh, is much like it was when the child was alive five years ago. The grief therapist was concerned that this preserved bedroom was a signal that this family may not be progressing with a healthy process of mourning. She asked the grief consultant, "Is this normal?" The grief consultant replied, "I don't know." Why does the grief consultant not know? To diagnose if this preserved bedroom is healthy or unhealthy for this family would require more information. The goal would be to ascertain if this family was utilizing this room to progress through the tasks of healthy mourning or if they may be attaching destructive magical thought to this preserved bedroom that would foster unhealthy mourning. Consider these two possibilities:

A Healthy Possibility WITHOUT Magical Thought

This family could be utilizing this preserved bedroom to progress with the tasks of healthy mourning without the existence of destructive magical thought.

Task I: To accept the reality of the loss

If one of the surviving brothers goes into this preserved bedroom and sees everything in its place and for that brother the preserved bedroom acts as a visual cue that his brother is dead, the bedroom helps advance the reality that the dead brother is dead. The surviving brother may realize his dead brother's objects are there (his brother once existed), but it is obvious his dead brother is not there (he is dead). If this is the case, the preserved bedroom is acting as a visual cue helping the surviving brother realize that his brother is dead. This would suggest that the surviving brother is progressing through Task I, as the preserved bedroom is fostering the acceptance of the reality of his brother's death. The death of his brother is a reality he accepts and he does not attach destructive magical thought.

Task II: To work through to the pain of grief

When this surviving brother visits his dead brother's preserved bedroom and realizes his brother is dead, there may be times when the surviving brother may experience the normal grief emotions: anguish, anger, longing, pining, commotion, etc. If this occurs, the surviving brother is feeling the emotional pain of grief, which is consistent with progression through Task II. His expression of his normal grief emotions is not being inhibited by the attachment of destructive magical thought.

Task III: To adjust to the environment in which the deceased is missing

The surviving brother visits the preserved bedroom. He realizes his brother is dead and he feels the various emotions of grief. He goes to face his school environment where everyone also realizes his brother is dead, which creates a better fit for him in his environment. To assist the surviving brother, the school social worker helps him develop a safe spot where the boy can choose to go to when he feels overwhelmed by his process of mourning. The safe spot gives the surviving brother empowerment by offering him a choice to express his mourning in front of others or to have a private time. The surviving brother visits the preserved bedroom which assists him in realizing his brother is dead, and others at school realize the impact of the death. They all make adjustments (developing a safe spot) allowing the surviving brother to have a better opportunity to adjust to his school environment, which is consistent with progressing through Task III. His ability and willingness to adapt to his environment and to work cooperatively with the school social worker has not been damaged by destructive magical thought.

Task IV: To withdraw emotional energy and reinvest it in another relationship

A major activity of this task is to invest in other people without "people replacing." People replacing consists of forcing others to be exactly like the dead loved one. Instead of attempting to "people replace," the surviving brother may take trusted family members or friends in this preserved bedroom. They may talk about the anguish, pining, and various grief emotions he has been feeling, which results in the strengthening of their bond. The surviving brother may invest into a support group and talk about experiencing the emotions of anguish and pining when in this preserved bedroom. If this occurs, the surviving brother is utilizing the preserved bedroom by investing in other relationships which reflects Task IV. His willingness to invest in other relationships has not been damaged by destructive magical thought.

Task V: To convert the relationship with the deceased from one of presence to a relationship of memory

This task requires establishing a relationship with the accurate and complete memory of the dead person—no editing the bad memories. Every good and bad part of the dead person needs to be recalled. As the surviving brother engages with his dead brother's objects in this preserved bedroom, the objects help the surviving brother remember fond times as well as bad times when his dead brother was alive. The entire family may converse together while sitting in this preserved bedroom, recalling the neat qualities as well as the aggravating qualities of the dead child. If a complete memory of this dead brother is promoted, the surviving brother and family are utilizing this preserved bedroom to progress through Task V. They are recalling the entire person and not editing and they are not creating a glorified version of the dead brother's memory, laced with destructive magical thought.

An Unhealthy Possibility WITH Destructive Magical Thought

Children and/or families could apply destructive magical thought to this dead brother's preserved bedroom to divert themselves from the tasks of healthy mourning by creating a shrine. When children experience an unhealthy process of mourning, their clinical issues can be uncovered by identifying their destructive magical thought.

Task I: To accept the reality of the loss

The surviving brother may use this preserved bedroom as a shrine. He goes into this bedroom and engages with the dead bother's objects while pretending the dead brother is alive. If this is the case, his activity, designed to preserve the dead brother's bedroom, suggests that the surviving brother is progressing, not with the tasks of healthy mourning, but with the Model of Magical Thought. His magical thought is assisting him to believe, "I can have my dead brother back by pretending he is alive when I engage with my dead brother's objects in his room." The surviving brother's progression with Task I (realizing his brother is dead) has been damaged by his magical thought.

Task II: To work through to the pain of grief

The surviving brother uses his dead brother's preserved bedroom more frequently when the surviving brother feels the initial presence of the normal grief emotions. When normal grief emotions arise, the surviving brother persists, pretending more intensely that his dead brother is alive, which allows the surviving brother to push away his normal grief emotions. The surviving brother has the magical thought, "If I pretend my brother is alive, I can avoid the emotional pain of grief." The surviving brother is using this preserved bedroom as a shrine to stop progression through Task II, as the Model of Magical Thought has damaged his progress with Task II.

Task III: To adjust to the environment in which the deceased is missing

The surviving brother is pretending his dead brother is alive and the surviving brother has accepted a magical thought to not feel the pain of grief, by pretending his brother is alive. The surviving brother goes to school where everyone realizes his brother is dead. He sees his dead brother's friends, which reminds him that his brother is dead. This dynamic stops the surviving brother from fitting in with others in his school environment. He starts to avoid going to school to maintain the pretense that his dead brother is alive. The social worker offers him an opportunity to develop a safe spot but he does not see the need for it, because his destructive magical thought tells him that he can get his dead brother back by continuing to pretend with his dead brother's objects. The surviving brother is not adjusting to his school environment. He has the magical thought, "If I pretend my brother is alive, he is alive" so the surviving brother must avoid environments or assistance that suggest otherwise. His lack of adjusting to his school environment is counter to Task III, as the Model of Magical Thought has damaged progress with this task.

Task IV: To withdraw emotional energy and reinvest it in another relationship

The surviving brother is pretending his dead brother is alive and avoiding family and friends who suggest otherwise. He starts to isolate himself so he can better maintain his magical thought, designed to enhance his pretending relationship with his dead brother. Due to his isolation, he is not investing in other relationships. His magical thought is, "If I isolate myself, I can be with my brother more often and I can avoid suggestions that he is really dead." His magical thought is counter to Task IV which suggests that bereaved children still feel love for the dead person, but cannot maintain an active relationship with a dead person. Isolation, based on magical thought, stops the surviving brother from investing in other relationships, inhibiting progression through Task IV. The Model of Magical Thought has damaged his progress with Task IV.

Task V: To convert the relationship with the deceased from one of presence to a relationship of memory

A qualifier for this task is that children need to recall all the positive and negative aspects of the dead person. Children who shrine dead relatives and pretend the dead person is alive often recall only a glorified portion of memory regarding the dead person, editing the negative but real aspects of the dead person. The surviving brother, who only focuses on the positive aspects of his dead brother, never considering the dead brother's negative qualities which foster his magical thought, "I am a good brother if I only look at the positive aspects of my dead brother." This magical thought edits reality, affecting the surviving brother's ability to have an accurate memory of his dead loved one. The Model of Magical Thought has damaged Task V because the surviving brother is editing truth and reality.

CONVERSION FROM THE UNHEALTHY MODEL OF MAGICAL THOUGHT TO THE TASKS OF HEALTHY MOURNING

Conversion Defined

This author defines conversion as the therapeutic process of assisting children and families to relinquish existing complicated mourning by eliminating magical thought and by rehearsing and implementing behavior consistent with the tasks of healthy mourning.

In this case, as the surviving brother uses the preserved bedroom to apply destructive magical thought, he may become oppositional to anyone who wants to pack up these enshrined objects. He needs these objects to maintain his deeply invested magical thought regarding his dead brother. Would the plan of action be the eventual packing up of these objects? No! What would be a plan of action that might create less resistance and still be quite effective? Conversion!

Instead of having the therapeutic goal of eventually finding that "right time" to pack up this preserved bedroom, a grief therapist can help *convert the purpose of this preserved bedroom to make the bedroom a tool which will assist the surviving brother in progressing through the tasks of healthy mourning.* This preserved bedroom can also function as a *barometer*. When the surviving brother no longer needs the dead brother's preserved bedroom and concludes it is time to pack up its contents, the preserved bedroom has the potential to act as a natural barometer indicating that progress with the tasks of healthy mourning has been made. Interference (suggesting that the family pack up the room or setting a timeline to do so) could destroy a very important barometer. Converting the purpose of this preserved bedroom allows the continuation of a natural barometer, but also encourages progression through the tasks of healthy mourning and the elimination of destructive magical thought.

One possible therapeutic activity, involving the surviving brother and the preserved bedroom laced with magical thought, would be to convert the preserved bedroom into a healthy component reflecting the tasks of healthy mourning. The grief therapist could reassure the surviving brother that there is no hidden goal—the grief therapist does not intend to entice this family into packing up the contents of this preserved bedroom. The grief therapist could suggest that this bedroom is very important and it could be helpful with the surviving brother's progression of healthy mourning. Many creative suggestions, to utilize this preserved bedroom by eliminating destructive magical thought and to convert the bedroom to reflect the tasks of healthy mourning, could be offered to the surviving brother. Consider the following suggestions for this boy.

SUGGESTIONS OF CONVERSION

Treatment

Suggestion 1

"Make a huge sign. A sign so large that it covers the bed in your dead brother's bedroom. The sign should say, 'My brother is dead.' Now when you go in this bedroom look at your brother's stuff, but also look at the sign."

The reality of this sign would advocate the elimination of the surviving brother's magical thought, "I can keep my brother alive by pretending with his possessions that he is alive." The sign says to the surviving brother that his brother is dead. The sign is designed to impinge on his destructive magical thought and enhance progress with Task I (to accept the reality of the loss). This therapeutic activity is advocating for Task I.

Suggestion 2

"Add a feeling poster (a poster with many facial expressions of emotions) to your dead brother's bedroom. Go into his bedroom and think about your brother. Look at the sign (My brother is dead) and then look at the feelings poster and point to the emotion(s) that you feel, knowing that your brother is dead."

This suggestion would advocate for the elimination of the surviving brother's magical thought, "If I pretend my brother is alive, I do not have to feel grief emotions." The poster in this preserved bedroom offers emotions, which may impinge on the surviving brother's destructive magical thought and enhance progress with Task II (to work through the pain of grief). This therapeutic activity is advocating for Task II.

Suggestion 3

"Make a safe spot in your dead brother's bedroom that you can go to whenever you feel overwhelmed by the emotions of grief or need to feel safe."

This suggestion of a safe spot would allow a conversion of the preserved bedroom from being a place of avoidance to a place where emotions can surface and/or be expressed. Safe spots developed at his school would allow for assistance with the adjustment to the environment where the deceased person is missing, eliminating the magical thought, "I do not have to adjust to my environment because he is not dead." A safe spot offers a tool for the surviving brother to adjust to the environment where the deceased is missing, which may impinge on his destructive magical thoughts and enhance progress with Task III (to adjust to the environment where the deceased is missing). This therapeutic technique is advocating for Task III.

Suggestion 4

"Take a trusted family member (a favorite aunt, uncle, parent, grandparent) and friends in your dead brother's bedroom and tell them all about this bedroom. Show her your favorite objects and the big sign on the bed. Show them the poster of emotions and point out which facial expressions show the emotions you feel."

This suggestion helps eliminate the magical thought, "I do not have to invest in other relationships because I can pretend my brother is alive." The surviving brother is being directed to utilize this preserved bedroom to emotionally invest in other important relationships which helps decrease isolation. Using the preserved bedroom in this manner impinges on destructive magical thought and enhances progress with Task IV (to withdraw emotional energy and reinvest it in another relationship). This therapeutic activity is advocating for Task IV.

Suggestion 5

"Let's make two cardboard figures of your brother that you can keep in his bedroom. On one cardboard figure, write down or make pictures of all the things you can remember that you liked about your brother. On the other cardboard figure, write down or make pictures of all the things you did not like about your brother. Ask your parents, siblings, friends, relatives to do the same on these two cardboard figures. Keep these cardboard figures in your dead brother's bedroom."

This therapeutic activity helps eliminate the surviving brother's magical thought, "My dead brother was only good and never bad." If the surviving brother edits memory of the dead loved one, there is greater opportunity for destructive magical thought as the surviving brother is not processing all of reality. Offering cardboard figures, with positive and negative aspects of the dead person, that can be stored in the preserved bedroom promotes accurate memories that impinges on the surviving brother's magical thought and enhances a complete and accurate memory of his dead brother. This therapeutic activity is advocating for Task V (establishing a relationship with the memory of the dead person).

EXAMPLE 2

In this case a girl internally dialogues with her dead father. She tells her grief therapist, "I talk to my dad in my head all the time." This girl is trying to determine if her internal talk with father is healthy. With the Model of Magical Thought, the grief therapist can now help this girl determine if her internal dialogue with the dead father is healthy or not.

A Healthy Possibility WITHOUT Magical Thought

This girl can use her dialogue with her dead father to help her progress through the tasks of healthy mourning, if there is no destructive magical thought damaging her progress with the tasks of healthy mourning.

Task I: To accept the reality of the loss

Could there be a healthy meaning to this girl's internal dialogue that could help her realize her father is dead? One of the reasons that children dialogue with a dead parent is to help them recall and keep the values of the dead parent. As this girl progresses with her mourning, she may recall and maintain some of the values of her dead father while accepting that her father is no longer physically available, which could be an outcome reflecting Task I—realizing her father is dead. "Dad is dead, but I still have retained some of the values that he taught me." This realization enhances her acceptance of reality of her father's death and maintains the separate identity of this girl, which is consistent with Task I.

Task II: To work through the pain of grief

If this girl discusses her grief emotions in her dialog with her father, she is progressing through Task II and if she eventually shares her grief emotions with others, she is progressing through Task IV. In this particular case, Task IV becomes an important factor in maintaining a healthy progression through Task II. Please see Task IV below.

*Task III: To adjust to the environment in
        which the deceased is missing*

As this girl internally dialogs with her dead father regarding current issues and problems, she may recall what her father would advise when problems occur. Her internal dialogue with her father may help this girl make better decisions, which would allow for a better adjustment to her environment. For example, if there was a conflict on the playground, she may recall previous conversations with her father suggesting that she should go to an adult for assistance. Instead of relying on violence, when there is a conflict on the playground, this girl follows her father's remembered advice and gets the assistance of a teacher which allows her to make a better adjustment to her environment.

*Task IV: To withdraw emotional energy and
        reinvest it in another relationship*

All of the tasks are important, but in some cases particular tasks are quite important. In this case, Task IV is quite important as Task II (in her case, talking to her dead father about grief emotions) by itself may eventually become destructive. One endeavor that fosters Task IV is investing in other people. When this girl told her grief therapist that she talked to her dead father, she invested in other people as she shared a very personal issue with her grief therapist. The grief therapist could assist this girl to invest in others by having her talk to other trusted people about her dialoguing with her dead father. "Could you talk to Grandma, Mom, or others about talking to dead dad?" The grief therapist is taking the girl's initial investment in the grief therapist and attempting to spread the girl's investment to other people who are important to this girl.

Task V: To convert the relationship with the deceased from one of presence to a relationship of memory

If through these conversations this girl remembers the positive and negative aspects of her dead father, her internal dialogue is helping her progress through Task V.

An Unhealthy Possibility WITH Magical Thought

This girl could alter her internal dialogue with her dead father by applying destructive magical thought to pervert the purpose of this internal dialogue, resulting in an unhealthy process of mourning.

Task I: To accept the reality of the loss

Whenever faced with the reality that her father is dead, this girl isolates herself and internally talks to her dead father, convincing herself that her father is alive. Her dysfunctional behavior is based on her magical thought, "If I can talk to my dad in my head, he is not dead." Her denial of her father's death is supported by this destructive magical thought and is stopping progress through Task I.

Task II: To work through the pain of grief

Whenever her normal grief emotions come to this girl, she isolates herself and internally talks to her dead father, which pushes away her normal grief emotions. She harbors the magical thought, "I do not have to feel the emotions of grief, as my dad is not dead if I can talk to him in my head." Her magical thought directs this girl away from progressing with Task II.

Task III: To adapt to the environment in which the deceased is missing

This girl develops beyond internal dialogue, openly talking to her dead father in class which causes her classmates to ridicule her. A school social worker may offer this girl a safe spot, but the girl does not use the safe spot because she does not perceive that her father is dead. She may have a magical thought such as, "If my dad is with me in my head, I do not need to adapt to my environment because a loss has not occurred." Her magical thought is assisting with the development of an unhealthy process of mourning and inhibiting her progress with Task III.

Task IV: To withdraw emotional energy and reinvest it in another relationship

Instead of investing in other relationships, this girl will only exclusively discuss her grief emotions internally with her dead father. Or she believes she does not have grief emotions because she converses only with her father, as the girl's magical thought has convinced her that her father is not dead. She has the magical thought, "My dad is alive and I don't need to talk to anyone else." This magical thought is counter to Task IV because this girl does not feel a need to invest in other relationships to fill the void of her dead father, due to her belief that she still has access to her father.

Task V: To convert the relationship with the deceased from one of presence to a relationship of memory

Establishing a relationship with the memory of a dead loved one is different than continuing a relationship through internal dialog with a dead loved one. This girl has not established a relationship with the accurate memory of her father. She is attempting to continue a relationship with her father by using her memories to interact with her father as if her father was still alive. Her magical thought that she has access to her real father, inhibits her progress of establishing a relationship with the memory of her father, which is damaging her progress through Task V.

SUGGESTIONS OF CONVERSION

Treatment

Many creative suggestions could be offered to this girl who is using this type of internal dialogue coupled with destructive magical thought to digress from a healthy process of mourning. Consider the following suggestions:

Suggestion 1

A grief therapist could have therapy sessions with this girl at the graveside of the girl's dead father. During therapy sessions the grief therapist could associate pictures of the dead loved one and the dead loved one's favorite objects with the graveside. The goal of conversion is not to stop the girl's internal dialog with her father. The goal is to gradually assist this girl to realize that her father is dead and that she can establish a relationship with the memory of her father. The goal is to eliminate the girl's magical thought, "If I can talk to dad in my head, he is alive," by associating father with his graveside to advocate for Task I—the reality that her father is dead.

Suggestion 2

Activities for Task II should allow this girl to feel her normal grief emotions. Since she is so focused on her internal dialog with her father, one possible technique to assist in eliminating her destructive magical thought is to have this girl draw simple pictures of the many faces of her father, each expressing a different emotion. These drawings could be posted in the room in which this girl tends to isolate. With adult assistance or instruction, the girl could be asked to point to the drawing that best expresses the emotion the girl is feeling. This girl is utilizing the various drawings of her father's facial expressions to express and associate with the normal grief emotions, which eliminates the magical thought, "If I pretend my father is alive, I do not have to feel the emotions of grief." This therapeutic technique is advocating for Task II.

Suggestion 3

In response to this girl's open dialogue with her dead father at school, a structured safe spot at school could be developed. She can be instructed that when she feels her grief emotions and/or wants to talk to her dead father (the caregiver should often refer to this girl's father as "dead"), then the girl could give her teacher a visual signal and go to the safe spot. This safe spot would empower the girl and allow her to adjust to her school environment, which is consistent with Task III. The girl could also have a set of Polaroid pictures of the drawings of her father's facial expression, which would allow her to transport this tool and give her the ability to express and associate with the emotions of grief. This therapeutic activity is advocating for Task III.

Suggestion 4

Task IV is an essential task when children are investing into a relationship with a dead loved one as if the dead loved one is alive. To assist this girl in investing in other relationships, which reduces an over-investment in a dead loved one, she could be asked to show others which drawings of her father best expresses her feelings. For example, this girl has safe spots developed at home and at school. When she goes to the safe spot, she could be instructed to look at the pictures of the facial expressions of her father that best describe her current emotional state. Then she could be asked to share her chosen picture with people she trusts. At home, she may share those pictures with her mother and trusted relatives. At school, she may share those pictures with her teacher, school nurse, or trusted friends. The goal is to eliminate the magical thought, "I do not have to invest in others, because I have my dad," by converting her investment into other relationships. This therapeutic activity advocates for Task IV.

Suggestion 5

For this particular girl, one goal is to eliminate the magical thought that memories of her father are equivalent to her father actually talking and engaging with her. For this girl it may be helpful to promote comparisons of people who are alive versus people who are dead. A grief therapist may ask this girl to describe (or draw a picture) all the activities that the girl can do with her mother, who is alive. The grief therapist could write a complete list of all the descriptions of the activities this girl offers that she can currently do with her mother. Then the grief therapist could ask this girl to develop a list of all the activities she can currently do with her dead father. The comparison of the lists will help this girl to realize the differences between life and death, as there are many activities with a mother who is alive versus a father who is limited to the activity of internal dialogue. Another version of this type of comparison is to ask this girl what her best friend can do with her father (who is alive) versus what this girl can do with her dead father, demonstrating the differences between life and death.

Another technique involves asking this girl to make a lifeline listing all the activities she did with her father when he was alive and to also develop a list of activities with father on the lifeline since her father's death. By creating these lists in concrete form, she can perceive that there was a point where her father became, due to restricted inter-action (no hugs, no playing soccer, etc.), a memory.

CHILD'S LIFELINE

<————————activities with dad—————————>(dad's death)<—>only memories of dad—>
_____
1 year 2 years 3 years 4 years 5 years 6 years 7 years 8 years 9 years 10 years

By listing the array of activities prior to her father's death, this graph highlights the notion that there are no new activities since her father's death except internal dialogue. The lifeline highlights, in con-crete form, that this girl is now engaged with only the memories of her dead father, as no new activities have occurred since her dad's death.

EXAMPLE 3

Bereaved children attempt to re-create what they had when their dead loved one was alive. Consider the example of a little girl whose mother has died. Her aunt (mother's sister) lives close by and after the death of this girl's mother she starts to spend considerable time at her aunt's house. She makes requests of her aunt to do the activities the girl's mother did when her mother was alive (make her favorite cookies, read her favorite story, etc.). Her aunt is more than happy to offer these activities for her niece.

A Healthy Possibility WITHOUT Magical Thought

Task I: To accept the reality of the loss

This bereaved girl wants to re-create the relationship she had with her mother, which is a normal aspect of grief. The girl's "attempts to re-create" are an opportunity for her to see the differences between her mother and surviving aunt and to realize that each has their own special and unique qualities. Without the complications of magical thought, she could easily realize these differences, which gives this girl a more comprehensive picture of the many facets of her mother that she misses. Her "attempt to re-create," without the complications of destructive magical thought, helps this girl to understand her mother's unique and special qualities. This conclusion is consistent with Task I.

Task II: To work through to the pain of grief

As this girl works through her "attempts to re-create" and her attempts fail, she realizes her mother is dead and cannot be replaced. Since she is without the complications of magical thought, she has easy access to the many normal grief reactions including commotion, pining, anguish, etc. She experiences her grief emotions and she consistently works through the normal grief emotions, which is consistent to Task II.

Task III: To adjust to the environment in which the deceased is missing

This girl's father and her siblings are also mourning very hard. She is overwhelmed by their grief reactions, which forces her to have many more grief reactions than the usual five to seven grief reactions per day young children typically experience. She visits her aunt to take a healthy break from her overwhelming grief reactions that occur in the girl's home. Her visits at her aunt's home allows this girl to get back to the usual five to seven grief reactions per day. Since she harbors no destructive magical thought about visiting her aunt, the visits help this girl adjust to her environment by giving her a place to take a healthy break. This activity is consistent with Task III.

Task IV: To withdraw emotional energy and reinvest it in another relationship

As previously mentioned, this task is often accomplished by children when they invest in other relationships that are unique and not involving a destructive magical thought such as "people replacement," where children pressure someone to be a duplicate of their dead loved one. This girl may develop a relationship with her aunt that is not a duplicate of her dead mother. She and her aunt bond with activities that reflect and blend each of their unique personalities which leads to progression with Task IV.

Task V: To convert the relationship with the deceased from one of presence to a relationship of memory

As this girl and her aunt develop a relationship, they discuss the girl's dead mother, which enhances an accurate memory of mother. As they talk and reminisce, they have no magical thought that her mother was perfect and they freely discuss the positive and negative aspects of their dead loved one, which offers a complete picture of what her mother was really like and allows this girl to progress through Task V.

An Unhealthy Possibility WITH Magical Thought

This girl may place destructive magical thought upon her relationship with her aunt, which would divert this girl from a process of healthy mourning.

Task I: To accept the reality of the loss

This girl could develop the destructive magical thought, "I can pretend that my aunt is my real mother." Then the girl asks her aunt, "Can I call you 'Mom'?" This girl may continue to offer a host of interactions with her aunt that reflect "people replacing," founded on the magical thought that she can get her mother back. If she replaces her mother, she has a magical thought that she does not have to accept her mother's death (counter to Task I) because her aunt *is* her mother. This girl's magical thought could stop her progression with Task I.

Task II: To work through the pain of grief

What pain? What grief reactions? This girl has the magical thought that her mother is not dead because she is busy making efforts to ensure that her mother still exists, by replacing her mother with her aunt. She does not utilize her aunt and her aunt's home to take a break from overwhelming grief reactions. Instead, this girl uses a magical thought to believe she does not have to have any emotional pain because her aunt is replacing her mother. Instead, she concentrates on getting her mother back by pressuring her aunt to be exactly like her mother. Her destructive magical thought may be, "I can avoid all emotional reactions of grief by pressuring my aunt to be like my mother," which is counter to Task II.

Task III: To withdraw emotional energy and reinvest it in another relationship

This girl can avoid making adjustments to her environment in which the deceased is missing by spending more time at her aunt's house, "Can I spend the night here?" Instead of utilizing her aunt's house to take healthy breaks, this girl applies a magical thought and uses her aunt's house to escape all grief reactions. She may have the magical thought, "I can leave my environment where my mother is missing and pressure my aunt to be with me and to be exactly like my mother." By spending as much time as this girl can at her aunt's house, she escapes the painful but necessary adjustment of her home environment where her deceased loved one is missing.

Task IV: To withdraw emotional energy and reinvest it in another relationship

This girl appears to be investing in other relationships but actually she is not. Instead of this girl and her aunt engaging in activities that they both enjoy and reflect the bonding of their unique personalities, this girl (using magical thought) is gradually and increasingly pressuring her aunt to be exactly like her dead mother. If her aunt is responsive to these demands, her aunt will become weary; their relationship will intensify and may disrupt. Her destructive magical thought may reflect, "I can get my mother back if I can force my aunt to be exactly like my mother." Her magical thought stops this girl from investing in other relationships and she never realizes the special attributes of her aunt, or the advantages of bonding with her aunt's qualities.

Task V: Establishing a relationship with the memory of a dead person

This girl does not establish an accurate and complete memory of her dead mother, because she is ingrained in magical thought intended to redesign her aunt to replace her mother. She has memories of her mother, but her memories are being transferred into an active relationship with her aunt via magical thought. She does not engage in establishing a relationship with the memory of her dead mother. Instead, she uses the memory of her mother to shape her aunt into being exactly like her mother. Her destructive magical thought may be, "When I reminisce about my mother with my aunt, my aunt will become more like my mother." The glorified memories of her mother now serve the purpose of offering a blueprint to her aunt on how to change to accommodate this girl's wish to have her mother back, which is counter to Task V.

Creative suggestions can now be applied to assist in guiding this girl back to a healthy process of mourning while diminishing her power-driven magical thoughts.

SUGGESTIONS OF CONVERSION

Treatment

Suggestion 1

Name replacement, which could lead to role replacement, should not be encouraged. With magical thought, this girl is attempting to blur the lines between her dead mother and her aunt. To allow this girl to call her aunt "Mom" may lead to the increased blurring of those lines and foster destructive magical thought. Her attempt to blur these lines by calling her aunt "Mom" may be one small step this girl is taking to deny the death of her mother. Her aunt could promote a healthy relationship by only being responsive to actual bonding based on the blend of their unique personalities or re-directing when this girl attempts to practice magical thought by making her aunt submit to the role of this girl's dead mother. By discouraging this girl from calling her "Mom," her aunt would help firm those blurred boundaries and reinforce the reality that this girl's mother is dead. This suggestion would also reinforce the idea that this girl's aunt is available and willing to have a unique relationship with this girl. This suggestion is counter to the girl's magical thought, "I can pretend that my aunt is my mother" and consistent with Task I (realizing mother is dead and not available). This therapeutic suggestion is advocating for Task I.

Suggestion 2

Instead of this girl's aunt attempting to replicate the activities and memories of the girl's mother, her aunt could be advised to demonstrate her own grief emotions about the death of her sister when the girl is present. The aunt's grief emotions are a signal and a reminder that the girl's mother is dead. The aunt would also model for this girl the expression of emotional pain involved in mourning a death, which is counter with the girl's magical thought, "I can avoid the emotional pain of grief by going to my aunt's house and pressuring my aunt to be exactly like my mother." This therapeutic activity would advocate for Task II.

Suggestion 3

It becomes obvious to this aunt that this girl's increasing presence at her home is a method of avoidance rather than a method of adjusting to the death in the girl's home. Her aunt may want to restrict (not eliminate) the amount of time she will allow this girl to spend at her home. This suggestion would be counter to this girl's magical thought, "I can avoid adjusting to my environment by leaving it and by going to my aunt's house and pressuring her to be like my mom." This aunt could spend more productive time helping this girl design a safe spot in the girl's home, which would offer the girl more empowerment and safety when attempting to adjust to the loss at home which is consistent with Task III. This therapeutic activity would advocate for Task III.

Suggestion 4

When this aunt and girl do spent time together, the aunt could be advised to reduce or eliminate activities that may suggest the magical thought that this girl is attempting to replace her mother. The aunt could include this girl in activities that reflect the shared interests of this aunt and this girl, not mimicking the shared activities of the dead mother and this girl. This suggestion will allow this girl the opportunity to develop a new and unique relationship with her aunt. Their new and unique relationship is consistent with Task IV and counter to this girl's destructive magical thought, "I can get my mother back if I can force my aunt to be exactly like my mother when she was alive." This therapeutic activity would advocate for Task IV.

Suggestion 5

Her aunt could be advised to occasionally review the photographs of this girl's mother and to reminisce with this girl. When reminiscing this aunt could talk about all the positive and negative aspects of this girl's mother, as well as discuss how the aunt and mother were different. The girl could be encouraged to do the same. This activity will help distinguish the boundary between mother and aunt as very distinct people, which counters this girl's magical thought, "When I reminisce about my mother with my aunt, my aunt will become exactly like my mother." This suggestion helps this girl keep an accurate and complete memory of her dead mother, which is consistent with Task V. This therapeutic activity advocates for Task V.

SUMMARY

These three examples demonstrate how children's grief reactions and management of grief reactions have the opportunity to become part of a healthy mourning process or could become part of an unhealthy mourning process due to the attachment of destructive magical thought. If a bereaved child is not progressing through one, a combination, or all of the tasks of healthy mourning, it is quite likely that the child has a destructive magical thought. Untreated, magical thoughts have the potential to develop lifelong patterns of dysfunction inhibiting the normal development of children's personality. Consider how each of the above unhealthy examples has the potential to disrupt children's personality development.

1. In example one, a boy uses his brother's room as a shrine. This boy learns not to progress with the process of healthy mourning by avoiding the tasks of healthy mourning and instead makes isolated shrines. He creates the destructive magical thought that when with the shrined objects he can pretend the dead person is still alive. What could potentially happen when this boy has another important person die or other types of loss occur? From his magical thought he has learned to isolate and pretend that the loss never occurred. However, he has to function in a world where the loss has occurred. This inconsistency is not a good fit with his environment. He has not learned how to progress with a healthy process of mourning so he is stuck in a cycle of isolation, non-communication, and the rejection of the reality of this death. He is very likely to develop defense mechanisms and/or personality disorders, which are counter to the development of an actualized personality.

2. In example two, a girl isolates when she dialogs with her dead father. She relies on internalized discussions with her dead father and never shares any emotional issues with others. She is now forty-five years old and even though that line between she and her dad's thoughts has blurred, one element survived—not talking to others. She has learned to shut others out of her life by neglecting to invest in other relationships. This isolation inhibits her coping skills, communication skills, assertiveness skills, and self-concept—the skills that assist with personality development.

3. In example three, the girl becomes obsessed with people replacement and as an adult may develop relationships with the intent of forcing others to be exactly like the original person who died. Instead of accepting and appreciating the unique features of others, she wants the original person back. She is so focused on finding a replacement, that relationships are continually destroyed as well as her own personality development.

SUMMARY OF THE MODEL OF MAGICAL THOUGHT

The Model of Magical Thought has several purposes and advantages to grief therapists, parents, and bereaved children.

1. The existence of a magical thought within a bereaved child is an excellent indicator that the child is not progressing through a task of mourning, a combination of tasks of mourning, or all of the tasks of mourning.

2. Realizing a destructive magical thought exists helps grief therapists and parents define the current clinical issue for treatment.

3. The goal of treatment is easily defined as eliminating destructive magical thought associated with children's process of mourning and to eliminate shared destructive magical thoughts within families. The goal of treatment also includes the development of adaptive behavior (behavior consistent with the tasks of healthy mourning).

4. If a child is progressing through the Model of Magical Thought, a prediction of the potential development of defense mechanisms and possible personality disorder(s) can be made.

5. Reading children's behavioral reactions can be a useful tool in determining children's magical thoughts. For example, when a child over-relies on a defense mechanism, the grief therapist and parents now understand that a child's defensive behavior could be associated with destructive magical thought.

PARENT SUGGESTION

The Model of Magical Thought is a treatment model that is designed for grief therapists. Parents are always cautioned not to attempt to perform treatment, as a dual relationship (parent and therapist) is quite complicated. Parents having knowledge of the Model of Magical Thought would be of great benefit in assisting the grief therapist who is assisting their children. An important role for parents is to assist children in making the conversion from destructive magical thought to getting back on track with the healthy tasks of mourning. Parents can keep a list of the tasks of healthy mourning readily available. Parents can use the tasks of healthy mourning as a guidepost. Whenever a bereaved child performs a behavior, parents can use the tasks of healthy mourning to determine if the child's behavior reflects a healthy process of mourning. If the child's behavior does not appear to be consistent with the tasks of healthy mourning, parents can assume a destructive magical thought may exist. Reporting a bereaved child's behavior that is inconsistent with the tasks of healthy mourning to the grief therapist would be quite valuable.

CHAPTER 5

Action-Focused Techniques to Eliminate Destructive Magical Thought

What are action-focused techniques? How are action-focused techniques applied to help bereaved children eliminate destructive magical thought? What are the advantages of utilizing action-focused techniques with children, adolescents, and families that are mourning?

ACTION-FOCUSED TECHNIQUES DEFINED

For the purpose of this book, an action-focused technique is any activity (psychodrama, sculpturing, behavioral rehearsal, etc.) that is designed to create an experience that will lead to discussion, which helps bereaved children and families to identify and eliminate destructive magical thought that distorts their healthy process of mourning. In other words, action-focused techniques are a variety of activities designed to help bereaved children and their families by converting their destructive magical thought into a healthy process of mourning.

ADVANTAGES OF USING ACTION-FOCUSED TECHNIQUES WITH BEREAVED CHILDREN AND FAMILIES

As a practicing clinical psychologist specializing in grief, I have found that action-focused techniques have offered tremendous advantages when treating bereaved children and their families. Consider the following list of very significant advantages to using action-focused techniques.

- One of the greatest advantages of action-focused techniques is that children can behaviorally express grief issues beyond their verbal abilities. What children cannot say with words, they can often describe by performing actions. Teenagers who have the capacity to verbally express can supplement their verbal expressions with action-focused techniques.

- Action-focused techniques can create timing. Grief therapists often attempt to determine the best timing to discuss therapeutic issues when utilizing therapies that rely on verbal skills. Action-focused techniques create timing by offering pictures and experiences that naturally lead children and families to a discussion of relevant grief issues.

- Action-focused techniques help children to adapt and assertively impact their environment. Children have incomplete cognitive equipment and cannot easily realize the many options they have available when processing grief reactions. Action-focused techniques allow children to discover the many options children have, which will help them process their grief issues and adapt to their losses.

- Action-focused techniques can be utilized to safely demonstrate for children the aversive consequences of their unhealthy behavioral reactions.

- Polaroid photos/videotaping can offer wonderful concrete reminders to children of what they learned from their involvement in action-focused techniques.

- Action-focused techniques can be used to uncover, reduce, and eliminate children's destructive magical thought.

- Action-focused techniques are children-friendly. Children enjoy these techniques which motivates children to stay in therapy.

- Action-focused techniques can be flexibly orchestrated with actual family members or substitutes can play the role of family members. This offers many advantages as the person who is dead can be in the action-focused experience by having a group member play the dead loved one to advance old issues and/or enhance the complete memory of the dead loved one. Another advantage of substitution is that children may feel less threatened when actual family members are not in the action-focused technique. Having the actual family members has advantages as action-focused techniques may offer a more complete and comprehensive picture of the dynamics of the family. Another advantage is that actual family members can participate together in rehearsing more adaptive behavioral options.

- Action-focused techniques are not dependent on having more than one person in therapy. When a grief therapist is offering individual therapy to one child, action-focused techniques can still be utilized. The grief therapist can have full size cardboard figures of a father, mother, sister, brother, dog, cat, etc. When a grief therapist is offering therapy to only one child, these cardboard figures can be utilized to create action-focused techniques.

FIVE PURPOSES OF
ACTION-FOCUSED TECHNIQUES

Although there are five ways to utilize action-focused techniques with bereaved children and families, when each of these five methods are applied in therapy they share the goal of eliminating and maintaining the elimination of destructive magical thought.

1. Action-focused techniques can create activities and experiences that children can use to concretely *demonstrate dysfunctional dynamics.* Recall the previously discussed story of the five-year-old child, Heather, whose grandfather was dying and parents were divorcing. She had the destructive magical thought that she had no power in her life, which impeded her progress with Task III—to adjust to the environment in which the deceased is missing. Her grief therapist asked her to be the director of a play to demonstrate the events that were happening when she would go to her friend's house. Heather's play included a re-enactment of "neighbor mother's" intrusions. By being the director of this play and thoroughly re-enacting the situation, Heather *demonstrated the dysfunctional dynamics* of that intrusive situation that was adversely affecting her. Her *demonstration of the dysfunctional dynamics* allowed the grief therapist to realize the full impact of Heather's situation and to assist in designing possible solutions.

Two boys who made fun of the fact that Adrian's father was dead were teasing Adrian on the playground. He had the destructive magical thought that he did not have the power to create a productive change. By re-enacting this scenario with action-focused techniques, he *demonstrated the dysfunctional dynamics* of the playground situation that needed to be addressed.

The purpose, of *demonstrating the dysfunctional dynamics* of grief-related situations with action-focused techniques, is that these techniques allow children to express more completely the issues of concern beyond what their verbal abilities allow. Action-focused techniques also allow grief therapists and parents to see a more complete picture of what a child is enduring and how a destructive magical thought is effecting a child's ability to adapt. This complete picture may also help the grief therapist consider more accurate and viable solutions for the situations that need to be affected/impacted, which could eventually or immediately eliminate children's destructive magical thought.

2. Action-focused techniques can be utilized *to rehearse adaptive behavioral responses* for bereaved children and families to help them eliminate destructive magical thought and to adapt to their environments. Five-year-old Heather, with the intrusive neighbor mom, needed to adapt by assertively impacting this intrusive situation so Heather could empower herself within her environment, allowing her to maintain her friendship with her five-year-old friend. She was offered several possible adaptive behavioral responses and she decided on one of the options which was thoroughly rehearsed. The assertive option Heather rehearsed was making a phone call to her mother and instructing the intrusive neighbor mom to address her intrusive questions to Heather's mother. She effectively rehearsed assertively redirecting adult issues to an adult. Her well-rehearsed adaptive option ended the intrusive questions and allowed Heather to have access to her five-year-old friend, eliminating the destructive magical thought that she had no power in her life. This *rehearsed adaptive behavioral response* helped Heather progress through Task III— adjusting to her environment.

Adrian, who was being teased on the playground, *rehearsed the adaptive behavioral response* of informing an adult of the intense teasing when it occurred. He also rehearsed a meeting with his teacher and the teasing boys to suggest that he did not want the boys punished, but wanted them to realize how hurtful they were when they teased him about his dead father. In the meeting, he wanted these teasing children to listen to how hurtful they had been. For example, one item he rehearsed was to tell them about a time when he had to leave his crying mother because he had to be at school on time. Then on his way to school these boys teased him. After the actual meeting, their teacher now had a sensitivity to his situation and observed it closely during recess. The boys stopped teasing him because they had a more complete picture of what he was enduring. Through his assertive actions these teasing boys also came to realize that important adults were aware of their behavior. The boys stopped teasing him and they started to include him in their activities.

The purpose of "rehearsing adaptive behavioral responses" is to offer tools to help bereaved children adapt to the changes in their environment resulting from a loss. *Rehearsing adaptive behavioral responses* allows concrete-thinking children to see more potential options when considering their actions and reactions to all the many new issues related to their loss experiences. *Rehearsing adaptive behavioral responses* offers children empowerment to adjust to their environment and to eliminate the power of destructive magical thoughts.

3. Action-focused techniques can be used as a *projective device* allowing bereaved children and families an avenue to express their grief emotions, as well as to express their distorted emotional reactions influenced by destructive magical thought.

When Heather was acting out the scenario with the intrusive neighbor mother, she exhibited considerable body language and facial expressions that *projected* emotional states. She also told her own mother, who was acting in the role of the five-year-old friend, how to act when the neighbor mother was being intrusive. She instructed her mother to act as her friend did, including facial expressions reflecting her friend's emotional reactions to these intrusions. Heather effectively demonstrated that her five-year-old friend was reacting emotionally with stress and frustration when the neighbor mother was intrusive.

Adrian was able to *project* his emotions when playing himself in the re-enactment involving the two bullies on the playground. His facial expressions indicated confusion and frustration. By telling the other two actors (who were playing the bullies), how to act like the real bullies, he demonstrated their emotional states which included those of scorn for him and delight when they were hurting him.

The purpose of action-focused techniques utilized as a *projective device* is that these techniques offer children the real opportunity to express and demonstrate emotions that they may not be able to verbalize due to limits in their concrete thinking abilities. Even though children think concretely, they can re-enact real concrete experiences that *project* abstract emotional states.

4. Action-focused techniques can be used to help bereaved children and families to realize that their *magical thoughts will not work*. Children harboring destructive magical thought expect a wonderful outcome. Action-focused techniques can be utilized to demonstrate the actual destructive outcomes that children's magical thought might potentially or currently offer. Children who have magical thoughts have unrealistic magical expectations. Children who have the magical thought, "If I am perfect, my parents and I will feel better" believe that the outcome of their magical thought will be wonderful. They expect that if they are perfect they will feel better. They do not expect the reality that they will "burn out" by entering a cycle of perfectionism that could eventually lead them to self-destructive behaviors (e.g.,

intense relationships, drugs, suicide, etc.). Grief therapists, using action-focused techniques, can create scenarios to demonstrate to perfectionistic children that their *destructive magical thought will not work*.

If Heather's (the girl with the intrusive neighbor mother) magical thought, "I have no power in my life," is left untreated, she may never try to empower herself. Instead she may develop dependencies on others. Through action-focused techniques, the destructive end results of dependency could be demonstrated, effectively convincing her that dependency is harmful to her and that dependency will not work.

5. Action-focused techniques can be used to create *symbols of resolution*. Children and/or families can create reality-based pictures and experiences using action-focused techniques of what it would be like if everything was fixed and they had no destructive magical thought influencing their process of mourning. With *symbols of resolution*, children and families are asked to create action-focused techniques (e.g., sculpture) of the current issues of concern as if it were resolved. Children could be instructed, "Make a still 3-D picture (concrete way of saying sculpture) of how you would like it to be if this situation was all worked out." This technique offers a concrete picture of resolution for concrete thinking children to experience and remember.

For Heather with the intrusive neighbor mother, her *symbol of resolution* was an action-focused picture of Heather playing with her friend without tension producing intrusions. *Symbols of resolution* can motivate children to continue to adapt to their environment by allowing them to see, in concrete form, the results of their new assertive actions.

For Adrian, the action-focused *symbol of resolution* he designed reflected seeing himself play on the school playground without the negative comments of the taunting boys teasing him about his father's death.

THE INTERVIEW PROCESS

A significant feature of action-focused techniques is the interview process, which offers the probing, questioning, and discussion that occurs after the action-focused experience is created. Three different types of interview can be utilized.

1. Discussion of Dynamics

Once a picture is created from an action-focused technique, any and all dynamics observed in the picture created by the action-focused experience can be discussed. Bereaved children and families can be asked to describe the dynamics offered by the action-focused experience. Grief therapists can point out any dynamics the action-focused technique uncovers.

2. Probe for Magical Thoughts

The grief therapist can explore and ask bereaved children and families if any destructive magical thoughts may be the catalyst for certain behavior that is reflected in the action-focused experience.

3. Realistic Concerns

Realistic worries and fears also drive behavior. Children and adults can be asked about realistic worries, fears, and concerns reflected in the picture that may be fueling their behavior, which was created via an action-focused experience.

Action-Focused Techniques Combined

Using the previous example of Heather with the intrusive neighbor mother, her destructive magical thought was, "I have no power in my life" which was effecting Task III—her ability to adjust to her environment. A combination of action-focused techniques can be utilized to assist Heather in eliminating her destructive magical thought. The first step in assisting Heather was to utilize an action-focused technique to have her *demonstrate the dysfunctional dynamics* offered by the intrusive neighbor mother. This was accomplished by asking Heather to be the director of a play and through the play she demonstrated all the intrusions she experienced from the intrusive neighbor mother. Using the action-focused technique as a *projective device,* she also demonstrated her emotional reactions as well as the emotional reactions of her five-year-old friend. Heather was able to express emotions in this action-focused technique that she could not yet express with words. Next, Heather was asked to use an action-focused technique of *rehearsing adaptive behavioral options* so she could gain access to her friend. She rehearsed making the phone call to her mother and giving the phone to the intrusive neighbor mother. This adaptive behavioral option gave the intrusive neighbor mother an adult with whom she could discuss adult issues, thus allowing Heather to play with her friend. Heather could also be instructed to make a *symbol of the resolution* offering the result she would like to have, which was playing with her friend without the tension producing intrusions.

Heather could also be asked to make a picture representing what would happen if she accepted her destructive magical thought (I have no power in my life) and did nothing to create change in this situation. An action-focused technique could be used to demonstrate to Heather that she would never be able to play with her friend, which would help her realize that her *magical thought was not working.*

In Heather's case, the five purposes of action-focused techniques were used to eliminate her destructive magical thought (I have no power in my life), which was having an effect on her progression through Task III—adjusting to her environment. By using action-focused techniques, her destructive magical thoughts dissipated as she learned that she could not stop her losses, which included her grandfather dying and her parents divorcing, but she could adjust to her environment. With the elimination of her destructive magical thought (I have no power in my life) she could now progress through Task III (adjusting to her environment) by rehearsing adaptive behavioral options.

PARENTAL INVOLVEMENT

One very common and practical question that grief therapists have regarding action-focused techniques is, "Are parents comfortable performing action-focused techniques to assist their children and how does the grief therapist suggest utilizing action-focused techniques to parents?" Most parents want direction with assisting their bereaved children and they rarely resist techniques that require activity. They are even less resistant if the grief therapist introduces action-focused techniques with a presentation that emphasizes the logic and practicality of this approach.

"The Presentation"

The introduction of action-focused techniques to parents works best when the grief therapist has a well-rehearsed presentation with the following components:

- Normalcy—The presentation should suggest that it is normal and customary that therapies for children include activities. Children need activities to keep their attention and to keep them engaged in the therapeutic process.
- Therapy for Children is Different—The presentation can suggest that therapy for children is different than therapy for adults. Children have incomplete and developing cognitive equipment.

They need activities to express grief emotions and describe situations that they may not be capable of expressing with words.

- Marketing to Children—Marketing to children does not mean marketing for money. Marketing to children means that grief therapists design therapy sessions that result in children wanting to come back and to continue grief therapy. When children are offered therapy as mini-adults (talk only), they tend to not want to come back.

- Activities Lead to Talk—Parents can be encouraged that talking is a very important part of grief therapy for children and that activities are designed to enhance children's ability to talk about grief issues.

- Timing—Activities lead to timing. For instance, once a picture is obtained from an action-focused technique, the time is right for the grief therapist to advocate a productive discussion of the picture.

Here is a helpful example of a presentation designed to help convince parents to become involved in action-focused techniques:

> Therapy for children is not the same as therapy for adults. If you have been to therapy or have an idea of what therapy is like, you probably anticipate that we will sit and talk to each other. Eventually, we will talk, but children have a lot of energy and just sitting and talking is difficult for them. In fact, it creates a very intense hour for children. After several sessions of talk, they tend to not want to come back. That is why it is helpful if we can do activities together first and then get to the talk we need to do. It keeps the children engaged and they tend to talk more after activities.

A presentation as this, in the grief therapist's own words, is very helpful in enlisting the involvement of parents in action-focused techniques.

PARENT SUGGESTION

Parents can have an expectation that therapy for children is different than therapy for adults. Parents can be open to performing activities in therapy sessions realizing that important conversations will result from activities. Children will follow their parents' lead. If parents appear comfortable with activities, children usually will also feel comfortable.

EXAMPLES OF ACTION-FOCUSED TECHNIQUES ELIMINATING MAGICAL THOUGHT

Sculpting/3-D Pictures

Virginia Satir was the enlightened founder of sculpting that had a profound effect of group and family psychotherapies. Listed below are two examples of utilizing sculpting with bereaved children who are engrained with destructive magical thought.

THE STORY OF JEAN

Jean was a five-year-old child whose father was killed in a car accident. Jean had a very good mother and her mother was intensely mourning the loss of her husband, but in a healthy manner—consistent with the tasks of healthy mourning. Jean's paternal grandmother (whose son was killed) was concerned because Jean's mother was mourning and grandmother perceived mother's grief as dysfunctional. Grandmother's solution was to try to protect Jean and to ensure that Jean was raised right, so grandmother wanted Jean to live with her forever. Whenever grandmother, mother, and Jean were together, grandmother and mother would become hostile and argue over where Jean should live. Although grandmother and mother were very concerned for Jean's welfare, they did not seem to notice the effect their hostile arguments were having on Jean.

Plan of Treatment

There are several immediate therapeutic goals for Jean and her family.

1. Jean needs to express the dysfunctional dynamics of her grandmother and mother's hostile arguments and she needs to project the emotions she is experiencing when her adults are being hostile.
2. All potentially destructive magical thought for each person in this situation needs to be determined. What magical thought is driving each person's behavior and/or what magical thought is developing within each person resulting from this hostile situation?
3. Which tasks of healthy mourning are inhibited by this family's anger?
4. What does a symbol of resolution of this situation look like?

Step 1: Use An Action-Focused Technique

Jean's grief therapist asked Jean to create a "still 3-D picture" (concrete expression for a sculpture) of what it is like for Jean when grandmother and mother angrily argue about where Jean should live. Jean made a sculpture with her grandmother and mother reflected in the picture below. Jean told her grandmother and mother to be real angry and to look only at each other. She instructed them to pull on her arms very hard in different directions with both hands (see Figure 1).

The grief therapist took a Polaroid photo of the picture resulting from the sculpture Jean created, which can be referred to later in the therapeutic process. The Polaroid photo of Jean's sculpture allows this concrete thinking girl to have a concrete representation of the picture she created with her sculpture. This Polaroid photo also allows defensive adults a concrete representation of the sculpture. Due to defensiveness, adults may miss what was offered in a sculpture and may need to review the Polaroid photo to gain further insights.

MOTHER   JEAN   GRANDMOTHER

Figure 1.

Step 3: Discuss The Dynamics in the Sculpture

The grief therapist can use the sculpture Jean created to discuss all the dynamics her sculpture demonstrates. Discussion of all of the dynamics within the sculpture can be used to create productive conversation and enhance understanding of the dysfunctional dynamics in Jean's sculpture (refer to Figure 1).

As the grief therapist reviews the sculpture, questions and comments designed to develop discussion with this family about the dynamics in the sculpture are offered. Consider these potential questions and comments to create discussion based upon this sculpture (refer to Figure 1):

"I wonder what it feels like to be in the middle of two big people who are angrily arguing? Grandmother and mother, have you ever been in a situation like this when you were a child? Do you recall what that feels like and what happened?"

"Did you see the emotion on Jean's face in this sculpture? What is her emotional expression saying to each of you? How do you think it would feel to have that emotional expression for a long time?"

"Did you notice Jean said 'pull hard'? I wonder what that means? I wonder what may happen if this continues for a long time?"

"Jean told you both to not look at her when you two are pulling on her and being angry? Have you noticed what Jean is actually experiencing when you two are actively arguing?"

"Does Jean try to keep you both happy when you are angry like you appear to be in this picture? What have you seen her do to attempt to calm both of you when you are expressing anger with each other?"

Many further questions can be offered to this family about the dynamics in Jean's sculpture to develop productive discussion. The reader is encouraged to develop further questions based on the dynamics of Jean's sculpture.

Step 4: Discuss Possible Magical Thoughts

The grief therapist can begin to ask about the existence of possible magical thoughts that each person in the sculpture may have that is creating a power-based catalyst reflected in Jean's sculpture. Consider the questions below to help generate discussion about destructive magical thought from Jean's sculpture:

"What power-based magical thought might Jean develop if she were in this stretched and pulled family position for a long time? Might she eventually conclude that to keep people together she needs to keep them arguing? Might she conclude that if she were gone that people would quit arguing, so she needs to eliminate herself to stop the arguing? Might she conclude that people are not happy when she is in the middle of them? Might she conclude that to keep people happy, she needs to stay away or eliminate her?"

The reader can consider how Jean's potential magical thoughts mentioned above may effect or eliminate the process of healthy mourning for Jean.

Below are examples of grandmother's potentially destructive magical thought from Jean's sculpture:

"What power-based magical thoughts are pushing grandmother to take Jean from Jean's mother? Might grandmother be considering that she could replace her dead son with Jean? Might she be thinking that her son did not die when he lived with grandmother, so grandmother needs to protect Jean from her mother? Might she be thinking that mother's normal grief emotions are destructive and that she needs to protect Jean from mother's grief reactions, stopping Jean from mourning? Might she be thinking, if I am over-controlling I am helping and Jean will want to come with me?"

Consider how grandmother's potential magical thought mentioned above may effect or eliminate the process of healthy mourning for this family.

What magical thoughts are pushing mother to pull on Jean and continue this angry argument?

"Might mother be thinking that anger gives her power which will help her keep Jean? Might she be thinking if people are out of my sight they will die, so Jean should never leave her sight?"

Consider how mother's potential magical thought mentioned above may effect or eliminate the process of healthy mourning for this family.

Step 5: Address Realistic Concerns

For the next step, the grief therapist can address realistic concerns that may be driving family member's behavior reflected in the sculpture. Once dysfunctional dynamics and possible magical thoughts are discussed, family members often bring up realistic concerns. Realistic concerns are actual reality-based fears and worries people have that drive their behavior. Often when families exhibit complicated mourning, their realistic fears and worries are not openly expressed. Jean's sculpture can be used to openly discuss realistic fears and worries by probing with the following questions.

"What realistic concerns, fears, and worries does each person in this family have that may be creating the behavior in this picture Jean created? Does anyone worry that this hostile argument may create another loss because these arguments seem to create separation? Does anyone worry that they will not be able to express healthy mourning, because all energy is saturated by this polarized argument to keep Jean? Does anyone fear that some day Mom may remarry and move away with Jean?"

Consider how the realistic concerns mentioned above could interfere with a healthy process of mourning for this family and each of its members.

From probing Jean's sculpture by suggesting and questioning dysfunctional dynamics, potential magical thoughts, and realistic concerns, a deeper more meaningful conversation occurred for Jean and her family. The following was determined for Jean's family.

Grandmother had two destructive magical thoughts. One magical thought she perpetuated was, "I could get my son back, if I could control and dominate my granddaughter." As mentioned earlier, if a destructive magical thought exists, it interferes with the tasks of healthy mourning. Grandmother had a destructive magical thought that she could "people replace" which is counter to Task IV—investing in other relationships and moving on. By using "people replacement," grandmother was attempting to use her granddaughter to replace her relationship with her son. Grandmother maintained another destructive magical thought, "Anger gives me power." To attain her granddaughter, grandmother used anger. If grandmother is only feeling anger and not the other emotions of grief, then her destructive magical thought is interfering with Task II—feeling all of the emotional pain of grief. Grandmother's destructive magical thought led her to believe that there would be a wonderful outcome—Jean would want to live with her. She believed that Jean would never have to experience the process of mourning, allowing them both to be happy and unaffected by this loss. Grandmother's power-based magical thought created behavior which resulted in attempts to eliminate Jean's mother and the manifestation of dysfunctional dynamics within this family. Grandmother also had a realistic concern creating more pressure within her to gain control of Jean. Grandmother realized that Jean's mother was young and attractive, and in the future Jean's mother may remarry. Grandmother had the realistic concern that if Jean's mother remarried, Jean may move away with her mother to a new locale, which would not allow grandmother to have a relationship with Jean.

Jean was developing a destructive magical thought based on being pulled into the middle (reflected in her sculpture) which was a very uncomfortable position. Jean was beginning to believe the power-based magical thought that if she was eliminated, the adults she cared about would stop fighting. Before therapy was initiated, when her grandmother and mother would argue Jean would run away and hide. Jean's power-based magical thought was, "If I am not here, they won't fight." Jean's realistic concern was that she was going to experience another loss if either adult won the argument. Jean realistically feared that she may lose another important adult in her life. Jean's ability to adjust to her environment (Task III) and invest in other relationships (Task IV) was inhibited. For example, she could not openly talk to grandmother about grief issues, as grandmother would use her comments as weapons against Jean's mother. Her environment was unsafe and her ability to talk openly was squelched.

Jean's mother developed a realistic concern based on grandmother's destructive magical thought. Mother was concerned that if she demonstrated normal grief emotions (Task II), she risked losing her child. Mother learned that she could not invest in her relationship with her mother-in-law (Task IV) by expressing healthy grief emotions, because grandmother viewed grief reactions as justification for taking Jean away.

Step 6: Plan Solutions for Realistic Concerns

It is necessary to develop solutions for realistic concerns. One realistic concern for grandmother, that was a major driving force of her behavior, was that her daughter-in-law may remarry in the future and move away with Jean. Real solutions and negotiation can be offered for realistic concerns. Mother and grandmother developed plans of how mother and Jean would always have contact with grandmother, no matter what happened in the future. This plan helped grandmother alleviate the fear of losing all contact with Jean.

Step 7: Switch Roles

The sculpture was redone and each person experienced playing the role of others. In this case, grandmother performed Jean's role in the sculpture, mother performed the grandmother's role, and Jean performed the mother's role. By switching roles, eventually everyone played all roles within this 3-D sculpture. The purpose of switching roles is that it helps to create empathy for what each person is experiencing in this conflict. Something very interesting happened in this case when grandmother played Jean in the sculpture (see Figure 2).

Notice that when grandmother played the role of Jean her stance was much more relaxed and calm than Jean had actually portrayed. When Jean had created this sculpture she told grandmother and

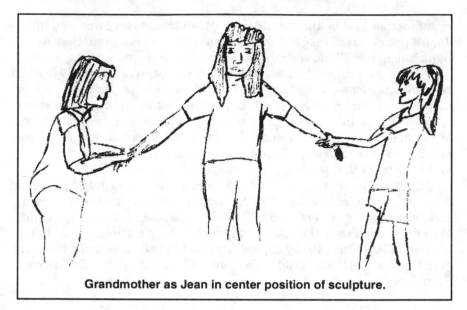

Grandmother as Jean in center position of sculpture.

Figure 2.

mother to look angrily at each other while they were pulling on Jean. By directing them in this sculpture she was saying, "When you two are angry, you do not look at or attend to me." When grandmother re-enacted Jean's position in a calm and relaxed manner, her performance suggested that Jean was right. Grandmother did not see Jean's anguished face because grandmother was focused on her anger toward Jean's mother, as well as grandmother's agenda. A Polaroid photo taken of the original picture of Jean's sculpture was offered to grandmother so she could see Jean's anguish. The sculpture was redone with grandmother playing Jean's role and accurately mimicking Jean's anguished face. When grandmother mimicked Jean's anguish, one of her destructive magical thoughts was immediately eliminated. Grandmother believed that her anger would give her the power to attain her granddaughter, thereby replacing her son. When grandmother accurately mimicked Jean in this sculpture, she felt Jean's tension and anguish. She also had the very important realization that Jean was leaning toward her mother. Experiencing Jean leaning toward her mother made grandmother realize the destructive effects that her magical thought was actually creating. Grandmother believed her magical thought would bring Jean closer to her, but she learned that her magical thought was not working. The reality that was offered by this action-focused technique demonstrated that grandmother's anger-based behavior, founded on her destructive magical thought, was driving Jean away.

Step 7: Create a Symbol of Resolution

This family was finally realizing the dysfunctional dynamics, realistic concerns, ineffectiveness, and destructive potential of their magical thought. The next step that they needed was a sculpture that offered a picture of healing and resolve. In other words, they needed a picture of a healthy resolution. Jean was asked to make a "still 3-D picture" (concrete way of expressing sculpture) of her family as she would like them to be. She asked them to get in a circle together to do a family hug. In the picture below, notice how Jean is linked to both adults (see Figure 3).

Compare this photo of the resolution to the original picture reflecting all the family's dysfunction (Figure 1). These two pictures created by Jean's sculptures offer strikingly different messages. Jean is saying that she cannot stand being torn apart by the two people she loves most. With her new sculpture, she appears to be expressing that she is the only reason these two adults are still connected. It is more

MOTHER   JEAN   GRANDMOTHER

Figure 3. Sculpture of resolution.

comfortable for Jean if these adults can exhibit behavior that reflects this new healing sculpture. The grief therapist can utilize this sculpture of resolution for this family as an agent of change for family dialogue and planning, as this new sculpture of resolution offers many healthy elements reflecting the tasks of healthy mourning.

Imagine the impossibility of trying to get five-year-old Jean to verbalize all that she offered with these simple action-focused techniques. Review again the therapeutic goals for this case:

1. Jean needs to express the dysfunctional dynamics of these hostile arguments and she needs to project the emotions she is experiencing when her adults are being hostile.
2. Their destructive magical thought needs to be determined. What magical thought is driving their behavior and/or developing from this situation?
3. Which tasks of healthy mourning are inhibited by this situation?
4. What does a symbol of resolution of this situation look like?

Each of these therapeutic goals was attained utilizing the Model of Magical Thought with action-focused techniques.

A FAMILY'S SHARED MAGICAL THOUGHT AND SCULPTING

It is not uncommon for families to share magical thoughts that can affect the progress of an entire family that is mourning. A family of six faced trauma when the youngest child (2 years old) was dying of cancer. When the doctor informed the mother and father their youngest child would die within one year, the mother developed a magical thought that was based on wonderful intentions, but became quite destructive. This was a healthy, productive, caring family and the mother was very concerned about the effect the dying child would have on her family. She stated her destructive magical thought in the form of a helpful suggestion with a wonderful intent that her family readily accepted:

> We have a nice, healthy, and productive family. To maintain this healthy family, I will take care of the dying child 100 percent of the time and the rest of you can continue to progress and be caring to each other.

The hospice volunteer, who was assisting this family, realized the destructive magical thought that the mother had implemented. The destructive magical thought had developed within this family for several months before the hospice worker made her observations during a home visit. Although the mother was under the impression that her plan was working, the hospice worker reported to the hospice's consulting psychologist that she was observing family dynamics that were quite dysfunctional and progressively getting worse.

Plan of Treatment

There are several immediate therapeutic goals for this family.

1. The magical thought, that a family can continue to be normal when one of them is dying, needed to be challenged.
2. If other destructive magical thoughts existed, they needed to be exposed. The destructive effects of each magical thought needed to be demonstrated to help this family realize that their magical thought is hurting this family.
3. The tasks of healthy mourning, that are adversely influenced by this family's magical thought, needed to be identified.
4. It would also be helpful to develop a symbol of resolution to assist this family in developing healthy goals with their process of mourning.

Step 1: Create an Action-Focused Technique

Each person in this family had developed a very isolated role within the family system that did not allow anyone to realize the full effects of their shared destructive magical thought, "If mom gives 100 percent of her attention to the dying child, we can continue to be a normal family." The hospice volunteer and the consulting psychologist decided to develop an action-focused technique of a sculpture, with the purpose of demonstrating to this family that their magical thought was not working. The mother and father had a wonderful expectation that their magical thought would continue the family's healthy development. Mother attended to the dying child 100 percent of the time and the rest of the family was expected to continue as usual, which inhibited a healthy anticipatory mourning process. The hospice volunteer described in detail to the consulting psychologist the reality of the dysfunction that she observed within this family that was based on the family's shared magical thought. Based on the hospice volunteer's descriptions, the hospice volunteer and the consulting psychologist developed a potential sculpture that they offered this family. Figure 4 is the picture that reflected the reality of that family's ineffective magical thought.

DAUGHTER   SON   FATHER   DAUGHTER   MOTHER

(The dying child could not be in the sculpture. The mother was asked to hold a satchel filled with books symbolizing the weight of taking complete care of a dying child.)

Figure 4. Sculpture of the destructive effects of this family's shared magical thought, "We have a healthy, productive, and caring family. Mom will take care of the dying child 100 percent of the time. The rest of the family is expected to continue to progress and care for each other."

Step 2: Take a Polaroid Photo

A Polaroid photo was taken of this sculpture. This Polaroid photo is especially important with this family. From observing the above picture, the reader can easily ascertain that certain family members have not yet seen the entire picture of the sculpture, due to their position in the picture. For example (refer to Figure 4), after completing the sculpture, mother's position indicates that she has seen the dying child only and not the entire picture, as her back is turned away from most of her family.

Step 3: Discuss the Dynamics in the Sculpture

This family's sculpture demonstrated that their magical thought was not working. The hospice volunteer and the consulting psychologist can now use the picture, created by this sculpture, to guide productive discussion of all of the dynamics of this family's shared destructive magical thought. Listed below are sample questions that may enhance discussion and this family's understanding of their dynamics based on their destructive magical thought.

The following is a listing of possible topics to discuss with this family based on the dynamics offered by this sculpture (refer to Figure 4):

"Why is the brother angry and pointing his finger at one of the children?"

"Mom has one of her hands up behind her back. Mom, what are you saying by having your hand up? Kids, what does Mom's hand mean to each of you?"

"Everyone appears so detached in this picture. Was everyone detached before the family realized this child was going to die."

"Who in the family has access to the dying child and who does not? Why?"

"Why is there a scapegoat in this family? What is the purpose of a scapegoat?"

"Why does there seem to be two separate subgroups in this family? A dividing line between dad and brother."

"What is the older sister trying to do with her parents? What has she identified that promotes this behavior? What does this say about the power-base in this family?"

"What does each person in this picture see? What does mother see? What does older sister see, etc.? Who has the most limited view? Who has the most complete and comprehensive view?"

The reader is encouraged to study this picture created by this sculpture to determine other questions and issues that could be discussed from this family.

Step 4: Probe for Possible Magical Thoughts

Questions for this family can now focus on the existence of any possible magical thoughts. The sculpture (refer to Figure 4) can be utilized to ask what individual and shared magical thoughts may be reflected through each family member's behavior. Consider these sample questions about magical thought.

"What other magical thought might Mom be harboring other than her family can have a normal life when a family member is dying? Might she believe that she can protect the rest of the family by stopping their grief reactions? Might she believe that if she can give the dying child 100 percent of her effort, she can stop the dying child from dying? Might she believe that when this child dies, everyone in the family will feel normal and continue with their lives, as if the child's death will have no effect?"

"What magical thought might Dad harbor that causes him to have his arms up between people? Might he believe that he does not know what to do, so there is nothing for him to do? Might he believe that he is helping mom offer 100 percent of her effort to the dying child by buffering her from the rest of the family?"

"What magical thought might the older sister develop as she continually fails in her attempts to bring her parents together? Might she develop a belief that she is responsible when others fail in their relationship? Might she develop a belief that if she is perfect, she will bring her parents together? Might she believe that if she whines enough, she can bring her parents together? Might she believe that it is her fault that her parent's have a detached relationship?"

"What magical thought might the scapegoating brother have that is pushing his need to create a scapegoat? Might he believe that if he becomes a parent for part of this family and keeps family members away from mom, he is assisting his mother with her 100 percent effort toward the dying child? Might he believe that he can vent all of his anger and frustration out on the most vulnerable sibling? Might he believe that if he blames someone, he won't be blamed?"

"What magical thought might the hostile scapegoated sister be harboring? Might she believe that the youngest children die first in this family, so she is next to die? Might she believe that if she wants mother's attention, she needs to be doing something extreme, such as opposition? Might she believe that she can help her mother by distracting the rest of the family from mother and the dying child?"

"What magical thought may the children in this family generate and utilize to get the mother to face them and interact with them? What magical thoughts are evolving about who is in control of the family and how control is attained?"

What other magical thought possibilities might the reader ask this family?

Step 5: Discuss Realistic Concerns

Realistic concerns can now be addressed which reflect the real worries and fears this family may share as well as those of individual family members. Their realistic worries and fears may also be driving behavior that is reflected in this family sculpture.

"What realistic concerns, worries, or fears does each person in the family harbor that may be creating behavior reflected in this sculpture? Does anyone worry that the family will break up after the sick child dies? Is anyone concerned that no one in the family has access to the dying child other than mother? Is anyone concerned with the need for a secondary parent (the angry scapegoating boy) and the effect of blaming the younger and most vulnerable child?"

What other realistic concerns, worries, or fears might the reader ask or address with this family?

From this line of questioning and probing, this action-focused technique has helped create a productive discussion about dynamics, magical thought, and realistic concerns, with a deeper realization of the adverse effects of destructive magical thought.

Step 6: Switch Roles

Because each family member is in very distinct and dysfunctional roles, it is difficult for them to realize the complete impact of their shared destructive magical thought and its effects on each family member. For this reason, each family member will switch roles and experience everyone's role in the sculpture.

Before describing the effects of switching roles, several magical thoughts were realized. The mother had a *surface magical thought* (openly stated magical thought) with a deeper magical thought affecting her intense desire to be constantly with her dying child. Her surface magical thought was that her family could have a normal life while a family member was dying, if she managed the dying baby with 100 percent of her time. The mother's *deeper magical thought (hidden or not realized magical thought)* suggested, "If I tend to my dying baby 100 percent of the time, my baby will not die." Since Mom had these destructive magical thoughts and no other family members had access to the dying child, no one in this family was processing any anticipatory mourning. In reviewing the original sculpture of this family, the mother has the most limited view—only seeing the dying child. The family member with the most complete view is the child who is the scapegoat. She can see her brother pointing his finger at her with anger, the father with his hands out, older sister trying to bring mother and father together, and the mother with her back turned and her hand extended behind her (see Figure 5).

As family members switched roles, the mother was eventually placed in the role of the daughter who was the hostile scapegoat, the family member who had a more complete view of the family. The mother's magical thought offered the expectation that her family should be having a normal life, but when she was placed in the role of the scapegoated daughter, the reality of the magical thought became apparent. Her magical thought was not working. The mother realized that their family life was not normal, as her magical thought suggested, which started to impinge upon her destructive magical thought. The realization that her magical thought was destructive to her family

**HOSTILE
SCAPEGOAT**

Figure 5.

motivated the mother to be accessible to other ideas that could help unite her family.

From switching roles in the sculpture, each person has an opportunity to gain insight and empathy for each person's position in the family. The father came to realize that there were times that he did not know what to do and there were times that he acted as a buffer to ensure that no one bothered the mother so she could give 100 percent to the dying child. The older sister came to realize that her father's goal of being a buffer was affecting her ability to unite her father and mother. She realized that she was not to blame as she and her father had different goals, which were, in effect, sabotaging each other. The older brother learned what it felt like to be a scapegoat and to have anger pointed at him as he was doing to his younger sister. Insight and empathy started to develop in many directions within this family system.

Step 7: Create a Symbol of Resolution

After insights were gained by discussing dynamics, possible magical thought, realistic concerns, and role switching, the focus of the treatment plan was directed toward resolution. This family was asked to create a sculpture of how they would like their family to be as this child was dying. They created a sculpture of the entire family, shoulder-to-shoulder, in a circle while they all together held the weight of the satchel (symbol of the weight of taking care of the dying child).

The original sculpture (refer to Figure 4) represents the results of a very destructive magical thought shared by this family, which forced the children to create roles without adult influence. Children were left to develop roles with their incomplete cognitive development. The symbol of resolution this family created together (everyone in the circle holding the satchel) had adult influence with a shared purpose—each person having access to the dying child in a united structure. The symbol of resolution offered a concrete representation of this issue resolved, which can be utilized to develop new and more functional roles for family members that are not based on destructive magical thought. Each child in this family could now develop roles that reflected the function of the sculpture of *resolution* (everyone working together with access to the dying child). This family created their sculpture reflecting resolution together guided by adult influence (parents), which offered more complete cognitive reasoning including abstract reasoning. When children are given a healthy structure (symbol of resolution) founded on more complete cognitive reasoning, they tend to develop more functional roles. This more functional sculpture of resolution was used to assist in defining healthy roles for family members. For example, one daughter said that she would make the mother a snack at night and visit the dying child while mother was eating. The other daughter volunteered to help the mother with the baby's diapers, as the baby needed to be changed quite often. The brother said that he would help his mother with the medication. Each child was allowed access to the dying baby and the mother realized that her destructive magical thought, of having a normal life when a family member is dying, was not promoting a normal and healthy family.

The mother had a deeper magical thought that was never addressed in this therapy session. Although she allowed her children access to the dying child, she still maintained the destructive magical thought that if she gave her dying child 100 percent of her care and time this child would not die, which was contrary to the reality that the child was actually dying. Even though the mother always had total access to the dying child, she was not progressing with anticipatory mourning because she was firmly convinced by this magical thought that she was stopping the child from dying.

Late one night, as the mother was tending to the dying child, the daughter who said she would make her mother a snack at night, made her mother a sandwich and a glass of milk. She brought the snack to her mother and gave it to her. While the mother was sitting by the sick child and eating, her daughter looked into the bassinet at the dying child and boldly offered this reality: "She doesn't look as good as yesterday." The mother looked into the bassinet and for the very first time realized that her child was dying. This interaction, based on a child's blatant truth, impinged on this mother's destructive magical thought that she was stopping her child from dying. This interaction was also the result of the sculpture reflecting resolution, where everyone in the family had access to the dying baby. Everyone in the family was now in the process of anticipatory mourning together.

PSYCHODRAMA/A PLAY LIKE A THEATER

Examples of Action-Focused Techniques
Utilizing Psychodrama

J. L. Moreno (1964, 1975, and 1969) was the creator of psychodrama, which has had a significant impact on group and family therapy. Consider the examples offered below of utilizing psychodrama with bereaved children who are deeply engrained with destructive magical thought.

The examples above offer helpful "3-D" sculptures, which are "still" pictures. Psychodrama offers movement and active rehearsal, which can be useful in eliminating destructive magical thought. A psychodrama is best described to young children as "a play like in a theater" which offers a concrete explanation and familiarity to children.

THE CLOSED DOOR OF DEATH

Karen was a fourteen-year-old teenager whose seventeen-year-old brother previously committed suicide. When her brother committed suicide, her typically stoic parents demonstrated a huge emotional reaction to her brother's death. She wanted her parents' emotional reaction for herself, but she was afraid to assert herself with her parents to attain it. She was very open and adamant about her destructive magical thought, which said, "When I kill myself, in death I will be able to see my parents' emotional reaction for me." Karen made several severe suicide attempts indicating that she was quite serious about killing herself to see her parents' emotional reaction. The grief therapist offered a question for Karen that often helps to impinge on children's magical thoughts about attaining emotional reactions after death with suicide. The grief therapist asked her, "How do you know for sure that you will be able to see your parents' emotional reaction after you are dead? No one has ever come back from the dead to tell us if this is possible." Often the insight prompted by this question will start to encroach upon a suicidal teenager's destructive magical thought. In Karen's case, she remained adamant that she would see her parents' emotional reaction when she was dead and nothing was going to change her mind.

Plan of Treatment

1. Reality dictates that no one knows what death is really like. What if Karen kills herself based on her destructive magical thought that she can see her parents' emotional reactions when she is dead and then finds that she cannot? Karen is concrete in her thinking and not considering other options, such as death could be a door that will not allow her to see her parents' emotional reaction. Karen needs to realize that seeing her parents' emotional reaction to her death may not occur.
2. Karen actually wants to see the emotions that her parents have for her. This could be accomplished by having this family utilize behavioral rehearsal to practice talking at an emotional level with each other.

Step 1: Create a Psychodrama Designed to Impinge on Karen's Magical Thought to Demonstrate that Death Could be a Closed Door

To assist with the first part of this plan, it was decided that a psychodrama would be utilized. The psychodrama would offer a concrete representation to assist in eliminating Karen's magical thought, which maintained that emotional satisfaction could be attained by watching her parents' reaction to Karen's suicide. Karen does not consider the option that death may not allow her to see her parents' emotional reaction to her death. A psychodrama was developed in which Karen would see death as a closed door, not allowing her to see her parents' emotional reactions to her death.

Karen was told that in this psychodrama, her mother and father were going to enact their mourning just as though she had died and they were attending Karen's funeral. Karen's parents stood in front of a table that represented Karen's casket and, when requested, they acted as though they were mourning Karen's death (refer to Figure 6).

Karen was asked to wait outside the office door. While she waited, she heard her grief therapist instruct Karen's parents to start mourning Karen's death, but Karen could not hear her parents as they were

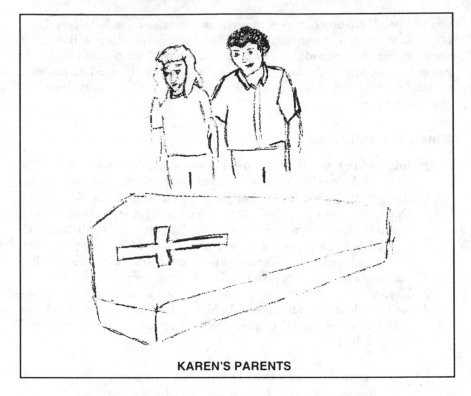

KAREN'S PARENTS

Figure 6.

actively mourning Karen's death. Karen opened the door to see her parents mourning (refer to Figure 7) and the grief therapist pushed her back and slammed the door and said, "You're dead."

Karen opened the door again to see her parents' emotional reaction, but the grief therapist slammed the door again and said, "You're dead." A third time an exasperated Karen looked to see her parent's emotional reaction to her death and the door was slammed again as the grief therapist repeated, "You're dead." Karen made eighteen attempts to see her parents' emotional reactions and each time she was frustrated by a slamming door—a concrete reminder that she might not see her parent's emotional reactions if she was dead. After eighteen attempts Karen said to the grief therapist with deep frustration, "You are trying to tell me that I am not going to see my parent's reaction if I am dead." The grief therapist replied, "That's right. How do you know for sure that you will be allowed to see your parents emotional reactions when you are dead?" This question, coupled with experiencing death in

KAREN ATTEMPTING TO SEE HER PARENTS MOURN AND THE GRIEF THERAPIST NOT ALLOWING HER.

Figure 7.

concrete form as a closed door, started to impinge upon Karen's destructive magical thought, "If I kill myself I will see my parent's emotional reaction for me." Maybe not!

Step 2: Behavioral Rehearsal to Promote Emotional Bonding

To assist with the second part of this plan, Karen and her family behaviorally rehearsed talking at an emotional level. Karen's emotional needs could be met and her parents could practice the type of emotional talk that they desired, but were never taught as children. Their behavioral rehearsal together strengthened her deterrence from destructive magical thought and enhanced their progression with several tasks of healthy mourning. As this family practiced talking with each other about emotions, they could more readily realize their grief reactions (Task II) and they could talk to each other (Task IV). As rehearsals continued and Karen's emotional needs were met, her need for this destructive magical thought dissipated.

EXAMPLE OF MAGICAL THOUGHTS, OLD WOUNDS, AND PSYCHODRAMA

Judy was a seventeen-year-old teenager whose father was dying. Her father had a history of being a workaholic and, in essence, had abandoned Judy in many ways throughout her seventeen years of life. Judy's father was rapidly approaching death and Judy wanted to have a very important conversation with her father before he died. Judy wanted to have an honest conversation with her father about his neglect of her and she also wanted to tell him that she loved him. Every time she attempted to talk with her father, she resorted to small talk instead of meaningful conversation. She had difficulties *making an effort* to talk to her father at any deeper level than small talk.

Plan of Treatment

1. Judy is blocking in her ability to *make an effort* to talk with her neglectful father. A psychodrama of a past wound may uncover and/or eliminate a destructive magical thought that might help unblock her effort.
2. Judy can behaviorally rehearse and refine with the grief therapist the desired discussion with her father about his years of previous neglect and also that she loves him.

Step 1: Create a Psychodrama of a Past Wound to Determine Judy's Destructive Magical Thought

When people who were neglected as children are asked to recall the incident they remember the most about their neglect, one situation from their many neglect experiences will often stand out above the rest. Even though the experience may seem relatively minor, the most remembered neglect experience usually has one major component affiliated with it. It is often the neglect experience that is associated with the death of the "fantasy parent." Children, such as Judy, will often have a long extended hope that their neglectful parent will change and become the fantasy parent they have always wanted. For many children, as cognition develops they will have experiences that help them realize that their parents are not going to change. When that realization occurs, the fantasy parent dies and children will often remember that particular neglect experience associated with this realization.

When Judy was asked the neglect experience she remembered most (when the fantasy parent died), she recalled a Parent Day celebration during elementary school. On Parent Day, parents would come for lunch and have a picnic on the school grounds. Usually Judy's mother would attend school activities, but Judy's grandfather was ill and her mother could not attend Parent Day. Judy's father promised Judy he would come for Parent Day and he would also bring her favorite lunch. Judy was thrilled because she believed her father would be there for her and she would get the fantasy parent she always wanted. On the way to school she told all her friends and bragged that her father was coming to school and bringing her favorite lunch. When she got to her classroom she went directly to her teacher and told her teacher how excited she was that her father was coming. She bragged that he was good looking, wore nice suits, and he was bringing her favorite lunch. Her teacher was very happy for her. Lunchtime came and all the parents came to class except Judy's father. One by one each classmate went to the playground with his or her parents, until Judy was sitting alone at her desk with her teacher sitting in the front of the classroom. Judy's teacher looked at Judy. Judy was so embarrassed that she opened the top of her desk, put her head inside of the desk, and partially closed the desk to hide her. At that point she realized that her father would never change—her fantasy parent died. The parent lunch was from 12:00 P.M. until 12:45 P.M. At 12:40 P.M. Judy's father came running into the classroom with no lunch and found Judy with her head in her desk. For the last forty minutes Judy had convinced herself that her fantasy parent was dead and there was no point in trying to have a relationship with him. For five minutes her father *made an effort* to get Judy to come out from under her desk so they could at least visit for five minutes. Judy refused and repeatedly shouted, "Go away!" He did. Judy developed a destructive magical thought, "If I never *make an effort* with my father, I will never be hurt by his neglect and his lack of effort." Judy convinced herself with magical thought that she could control the harmful effects of her father's neglect and his lack of effort.

In group therapy Judy was asked to do the above scenario in a psychodrama with Judy playing herself, a group member playing her teacher, another group member playing her father, and several group members playing classmates. The scenario was replayed in a psychodrama just as Judy had described it. The psychodrama started with Judy bragging that her father was coming and ended when he left after *making an effort* to get her to spend five minutes with him and her harsh refusals. After performing this initial psychodrama, no change in Judy's attitude occurred. For the next step, Judy was asked to play in her father's role in this same scenario, which included father's five-minute attempt of *making an effort* to convince Judy to come with him. After her fantasy parent died (when she realized she would never get the parent she wanted), Judy would never allow herself to feel her father's effort. When she performed in the psychodrama as her father *making an effort* for five minutes, she could feel his effort. This allowed her to *make the effort* to start to talk with her father. The truth of her destructive magical thought was exposed. Judy realized that her commitment to not making an effort founded on destructive magical thought was damaging and not protective. The truth was that dynamics had changed and dad was dying and he was ready to talk.

Step 2: Behaviorally Rehearse a Healthy Conversation with Father

Judy behaviorally rehearsed all that she wanted to say to her father by having the grief therapist act as her father. Judy could practice offering the effects of father's neglect without creating defensiveness. She could also rehearse how she wanted to express her love for her father.

SUMMARY

Action-focused techniques are any activities (psychodrama, sculpturing, behavioral rehearsal, etc.) that are designed to create an experience that will lead to discussion, which helps children and families to identify and eliminate destructive magical thought. Interview techniques include questioning and exploring dynamics within the picture offered by the action-focused technique, discussing potential magical thought of each person in the picture, and discussion and questioning any realistic concerns each person has that is within the picture. Action-focused techniques are effective in developing and rehearsing adaptive behavior (consistent with the tasks of healthy mourning) to replace the dysfunctional behavior (founded on magical thought). Action-focused techniques are children-friendly which create comfort for children and enhances their willingness to continue therapy sessions.

If these techniques are new to the reader, it is advisable for the reader to initiate using action-focused techniques in two ways:

1. Grief therapists can use action-focused techniques as a projective device. As a projective device, the grief therapist does not create the sculpture as the child creates the sculpture to project emotions and dysfunctional dynamics. A photo of the sculpture can be taken. Then the grief therapist can ask the child with photo in hand about dynamics within the sculpture, question the existence of magical thought, and discuss realistic worries and fears the child may be experiencing.

2. Grief therapists can use action-focused techniques to help children rehearse many adaptive behavioral reactions to grief-related situations. When children are not sure what to do in grief-related situations, rehearsal of optional adaptive behavioral reactions can be easily generated and demonstrated.

With any therapeutic technique it is important for grief therapists to receive training, guidance, and to read considerably on the topic. There is a tremendous amount of training and readings available and several are listed in Appendix A.

PARENT SUGGESTION

Action-focused techniques are one of many types of therapeutic interventions that are available for children with complicated mourning. Therapeutic techniques include play therapy, art therapy, reality therapy, expressive therapy, and much more. Grief therapists have an array of techniques for children that are active, engaging, and effective.

CHAPTER 6

Anger and Magical Thought

Anger can be an intense emotion that children, especially teenagers, may experience when a loved one dies. Children's intense and dysfunctional anger can become easily associated with magical thought, leading children away from the tasks of healthy mourning. Children may want the short-term effects of anger (reactions from adults, center of attention, button pushing, etc.) but not realize the long-term destruction that prolonged and dysfunctional anger actually offers.

Children and teenagers are unique in their expression of anger. Rarely does a child simply say, "I'm angry." Typically children express anger through their behavior. Children's angry behavior can function as a wonderful barometer suggesting the existence of primary emotions. This author defines primary emotions as those appropriate emotions that are consistent with the situation. For example, when a child is abandoned, a feeling of abandonment is the primary emotion. When a child is betrayed, a feeling of betrayal is the primary emotion. Primary emotions are abstract and children may have difficulty expressing primary emotions, but they know how to express anger through their behavior. Angry behavior is much more concrete than primary emotions and more accessible to children as they are attempting to manage their grief reactions.

Bereaved children may have healthy anger as well as unhealthy anger. For example, if a child's father is dying of cancer, the child may express anger over the situation that his or her father is dying. This child may believe that it is unfair that his or her father is dying and other children get to be with their fathers. This child is right, it is unfair; however, it is a reality that life is not always fair. This child's anger is healthy, logical, and not permeated with destructive magical thought or dysfunctional behavior.

Unhealthy anger derived from grief reactions has many varieties, but one of the most common reactions from children is anger expressed as a secondary emotion. This author's definition of a secondary emotion is an emotion that is not consistent with the situation, and is hiding the primary emotion. Secondary emotions are a signal that a primary emotion exists. In other words, anger can be a signal that a primary emotion exists. When a bereaved child has an unhealthy anger that is functioning as a secondary emotion (signal), the child is usually connecting a destructive magical thought to his or her anger which provides a power-based catalyst to continue the expression of his or her dysfunctional angry behavior. For example, a boy feels anguish and is angry that life is not fair because he has experienced the death of a loved one. He may add a destructive magical thought to the concept of fairness, "If I get angry, my mom should make this world fair for me." Instead of feeling anguish (a primary emotion), this boy uses dysfunctional behavior to angrily pressure his mother to make the world a fair place. The normal grief emotion of anguish and the unfairness of loss have now been blemished with a destructive magical thought.

Listed below is a prescription for treating children who have aggressive anger founded in the process of mourning, as well as the examples of "Andy" and "Patricia."

PRESCRIPTION FOR ANGER MANAGEMENT

Barometers
Target
Primitive Plan of Treatment
Identify the Primary Emotions
Symbolize the Primary Emotions in Concrete Form
Express Anger with the Symbol of the Primary Emotion
Treatment of the Primary Emotion

THE STORY OF ANGRY ANDY

Ten-year-old Andy was brought into counseling by his father. When Andy was nine years old his mother died of cancer. His mother was at home when she died of cancer as hospice was assisting this family. Several days before his mother died, Andy started to exhibit physical aggression. On his way to school, on the playground, and at school he was nasty, aggressive, and intimidating to all the girls at school. He was behaviorally appropriate with all of his male classmates. At school he was extremely oppositional to female staff, but he was his usual kind self when engaging with male staff. Through Andy's behavior, he was demonstrating significant anger solely toward females, which may be the result of a magical thought. Andy's angry behavior toward females can be classified as a barometer. Andy's barometer will assist in telling if a plan of treatment is helping or not. For example, if Andy is offered effective treatment to alleviate his anger, his behavior (less angry reactions toward females) will tell the grief therapist if a treatment plan has been effective. If a treatment has not been effective, Andy's angry behavior should remain constant or become worse.

Andy's anger toward females was very significant, but it was not the reason his father brought Andy to therapy. Andy went into therapy because his father witnessed an unusually compulsive and angry behavior from Andy. Andy noticed that on the inside living room door of his home there were two smudge marks, forming two dots at about the height of a person's eyes. Andy got a container of Playdough and rolled the Playdough into a hard ball. He started to throw the ball at the living room door with all his strength. His father watched this action and his father could hear Andy make derogatory comments about females. His father decided to let Andy continue this behavior believing that Andy may be releasing his anger. One and one half hours later, Andy's father had to physically restrain Andy from performing this angry behavior. Andy's compulsive angry behavior could be classified as his attempt to help himself—a primitive plan of treatment.

Consider the following structure for managing Andy's anger.

1. Barometers

Andy had offered a barometer that could be observed and quantified. His barometer was angry behavioral reactions toward females, which could be associated with magical thought. If treatment is offered and the barometer decreases or is eliminated, this may suggest that the treatment was effective. If treatment is offered and the barometer persists, the treatment may either be ineffective or incomplete.

2. Target

Andy had a target for his anger, which was the door. It was eventually learned that the two dots on the door were symbols of his mother's eyes. Andy was expressing anger at a symbol of his mother's face, however this was the first time Andy expressed anger toward an inanimate object. When he expressed his anger toward the target, he was not hurting anyone, which was a new and healthy behavior for Andy. Children without targets will often displace their anger, losing their original understanding of the issues that initially angered them.

By losing the reality of what generated his anger, Andy was more susceptible to the development of destructive magical thought.

3. Primitive Plan of Treatment

Andy had developed his own primitive plan of treatment. A primitive plan of treatment is often tied to a child's attempts to do Task III—adjust to the environment where the deceased is missing. A primitive plan of treatment is a concrete thinking child's attempt to develop methods to help him or her feel better. Andy's barometer was expressed in angry behavior toward females. With his angry expression at the dots on the door, which symbolized his mother's face, Andy was attempting to develop a new method for expressing his anger. Was it working? To determine if Andy's new method of expressing anger was working (throwing a clay ball at mom's face), the grief therapist only had to check Andy's barometer (anger expressed toward females). If Andy was expressing less or no anger toward females, his new method was working. If he was still persistent with his anger toward females, his new method was not working. Unfortunately, Andy's method was not working as he persisted in angry behavior exclusively directed toward females.

Andy's primitive plan to help himself was developed by Andy, who has incomplete cognitive equipment. There are parts of his primitive plan that may be quite functional. With slight modification of his primitive plan, his plan may become very effective. What has he developed within his primitive plan that is functional?

A. He is expressing anger and allowing his father to see his anger.
B. For the first time he is hitting an inanimate object. His new expression of anger is not hurting anyone.
C. He has a target, which could help reduce displacement of anger toward others, who do not deserve his anger.

These elements of Andy's plan can be modified and utilized offering a more effective plan of treatment. Modifying and utilizing what Andy has already designed suggests to him that he has empowerment.

4. Identify the Primary Emotions

Much of children's dysfunctional anger founded in the process of mourning is a signal that a primary emotion exists. One element that is missing from Andy's plan of treatment is the primary emotion that is fueling his anger. Concrete thinking children tend to not include primary emotions in their primitive plans of treatment because primary emotions are abstract concepts. Andy was expressing anger at a symbol of his mother's face (the 2 dots on the door were her eyes), which generated more anger as demonstrated by Andy's father who had to physically stop Andy's expression of anger—compulsively hitting the door for a considerable time. Andy was not ventilating anger. He was generating and rehearsing anger toward his mother and displacing anger toward all females. His displacement of anger on other females would suggest the existence of a destructive magical thought, such as this one possibility, "I can retaliate against my mother when I hurt other females."

If there is a primary emotion driving Andy's anger, he needs to be offered a method of determining which primary emotion is fueling his anger. Different grief therapists may develop a variety of creative techniques to assist Andy in determining his primary emotion. The projective technique called "fishing" was utilized for Andy. It is important for grief therapists to not assume which primary emotions are fueling a particular child's anger. Children are too diverse in their creation of magical thought to preclude anything. A true projective device is offered without any assumptions from the grief therapist. To use "fishing," Andy was asked to draw pictures of various primary emotions. Since Andy was ten years old, this request for primary emotions was offered to him in concrete form.

PRIMARY EMOTIONS

"Andy, for a moment think about your mother, now let's do this."

Abandonment

"Andy, draw me a picture of what it feels like when someone leaves you and you don't want them to leave."

Betrayal

"Now, Andy, draw me a picture of what it feels like when someone you trust turns against you and actively does things to hurt you."

Disappointment

"For the next picture Andy, I would like you to draw a picture of what it feels like when you are counting on someone and they let you down."

Helplessness

"Draw a picture of what it feels like when you want to change something, but there is no way to change it."

Embarrassment

"Andy, draw a picture of what it feels like when something weird or unusual happens and people pay attention to you, but you feel funny and don't want them to pay attention to you."

Hopelessness

"Draw a picture of what it feels like when you wish something would happen, but you know it is not going to happen the way you want."

Sadness/Depression

"Draw a picture of what it feels like when something happens and you feel very sad."

PARENT SUGGESTION

Parents can memorize and rehearse these concrete definitions of abstract primary emotions. Parents will be more effective when investigating children's primary emotions if parents have easy access to concrete expressions of abstract emotions. Anger can also be a very functional primary emotion (anger because the loved one is dead and it is unfair), but with anger as extreme as Andy's anger, it is often a signal of the existence of another primary emotion(s).

Adults, using concrete wording, can offer many primary emotions to children. An excellent way to ensure that a primary emotion is expressed in concrete form is by practicing saying primary emotions in sentences with simple words understandable to younger children. Another technique is to review a children's dictionary which will offer concrete definitions of abstract emotions.

Children tend to put considerably more effort into projective pictures of primary emotions, which are the emotions that are strongest within them. Andy's drawing of the primary emotion of abandonment was his most outstanding drawing. This projective technique of drawing primary emotions (fishing) assisted in identifying Andy's potential primary emotion (abandonment) which may be fueling his anger.

5. Symbolize the Primary Emotion in Concrete Form

Andy's picture of abandonment offers two functions. One, the picture has assisted in identifying a primary emotion, which may be fueling Andy's anger. Two, Andy's picture is a symbol of his primary emotion in concrete form.

When children are asked to draw pictures of primary emotions, children's drawings often reflect their current level of cognitive development. Andy was ten years old and of normal cognitive development. He was, at that point in his cognitive development, predominantly concrete in his thinking skills with early development of abstract reasoning. Andy's drawing of abandonment was concrete and yet slightly symbolic. He drew a slightly abstract picture symbolizing masses being pulled apart. Within his drawing of abandonment he also drew dark holes where people go and do not return, which was reminiscent of a gravesite.

6. Express Anger toward the Symbol of the Primary Emotion

Using all the functional qualities that Andy developed and adding the primary emotion of abandonment, the grief therapist can now

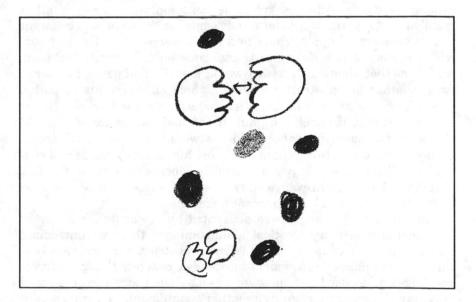

Figure 1. Andy's picture of abandonment.

modify Andy's primitive plan of treatment. From Andy's original primitive plan of treatment, the components that were identified as functional were his development of a target, his expression of his anger, his willingness to allow his father to see the angry expression, and the use of an inanimate object. One significant change that was offered to Andy was for Andy to erase his mother's eyes from the door and replace it with his drawing of the primary emotion of abandonment. Andy was instructed to express his anger toward his picture of abandonment, just as he did before with the two dots (Mom's face) on the door. Andy started to throw the clay ball at his drawing of abandonment. Instead of one and one half-hours of aggressive and uncontrollable anger, Andy's anger started to dissipate within a shorter period of time. The aerobic activity of throwing the ball at his drawing of abandonment appeared to release Andy's anger and his primary emotion (abandonment) started to surface as tears came to Andy's eyes.

7. Treatment of Primary Emotions

Since Andy's picture of abandonment seemed more outstanding than the rest of his drawings of primary emotions, Andy's father was asked if he could recall any situations where Andy may have felt abandoned when his mother was alive or when she was in the active process of dying. After considerable contemplation, Andy's father recalled that several days before Andy's mother died, she was coherent but in considerable pain. Andy and his father were in the bedroom where mother was suffering in tremendous pain. In frustrated pain, Andy's mother shouted, "I wish I would just die and get out of here." Andy's father has abstract reasoning, which enhances his empathy. When Andy's father was in this scenario he thought to himself, "She is saying that because she is in pain. If she had her choice, she would choose to not have this cancer and she would stay with us." Andy's nine-year-old concrete cognition processed his mother's words and concluded, "She wants to leave me." Andy's conclusion became the fuel that ignited a need for revenge and a magical method to attain revenge by displacing anger toward innocent females.

Now that Andy's anger was dissipated by releasing his anger at a symbol of a primary emotion (abandonment), the next immediate goal of treatment was to get Dad's more abstract and accurate conclusion about mother's statement into Andy's concrete thought processes. An action-focused technique such as a psychodrama can be utilized to replay the scenario of Andy's mother's statement, "I wish I would just die and get out of here." In the psychodrama, a female therapist played Andy's mother, Andy's father played himself, and Andy played himself (refer to Figure 2).

The female therapist (mother) said, "I wish I would just die and get out of here." Father (as himself) was asked to say what he was thinking and he said, "She is saying that because she is in pain. If she had her choice, she would not have the cancer and she would stay with us." That is the first time Andy ever heard his father's interpretation of this situation, which was quite different than Andy's concrete interpretation. Then Andy was asked to say what he was thinking when his mother made that statement. He replied, "I thought she wanted to leave me."

ANDY'S DAD   THERAPIST PLAYING   ANDY
                     ANDY'S MOM

Figure 2.

In the next phase of this treatment process, everyone was asked to switch places, resulting in Andy playing his mother's role, Andy's father playing Andy's role, and the female therapist playing the father's role (refer to Figure 3).

They were asked to replay this situation again. Andy was asked to repeat what his mother had said, "I wish I would just die and get out of here." The female therapist repeated father's interpretation, "She is saying that because she is in pain. If she had a choice she would not have the cancer and she would stay with us." Father repeated Andy's thought, "I thought she wanted to leave me." By switching these roles and placing Andy in his mother's role, Andy could hear and see the distinct difference between his father's conclusion and his own.

Another rotation allowed Andy to play his father, the female therapist play Andy, and his father to play in his mother's role (refer to Figure 4).

The scenario was repeated. In this situation Andy said what his father thought, "She is saying that because she is in pain. If she had a choice she would not have the cancer and she would stay with us." Not only did Andy hear his father's abstract conclusion (Figure 2) and see the difference between what he concluded and what his father concluded (Figure 3), but Andy (playing in the role of his father) could feel the words his father stated (Figure 4).

ANDY IN MOM'S ROLE

Figure 3.

ANDY IN DAD'S ROLE

Figure 4.

This psychodrama with these three rotations offered Andy a concrete experience, demonstrating father's more accurate and healing conclusion about Andy's mother's statements shortly before she died. Did it work? Andy's displaced anger toward females was his barometer. If his angry reactions toward females subsided then this three-part psychodrama was effective. Andy's angry reactions toward females and his need for revenge did subside.

PATRICIA'S ANGER DID NOT SUBSIDE

In Patricia's case a similar psychodrama did not appear to be releasing her anger and helping her cope with her father's death. Patricia's father had died and Patricia had a similar method of expressing anger as Andy, which was dysfunctional and included displacement onto others. A similar technique was offered to Patricia with all of the healthy therapeutic elements mentioned in Andy's case. Patricia's projective pictures suggested her most significant primary emotion appeared to be abandonment. She had a similar physical expression of anger as Andy, which was used with a picture (concrete symbol) of her most significant primary emotion—abandonment. Patricia released her anger at her symbol of the primary emotion and a psychodrama was developed to "clean up" her inaccurate conclusions. Great results were expected, but they did not occur. Patricia's barometer was still active as she continued to express her anger in a very destructive manner, actively using displacement to hurt innocent people.

What happened? Abandonment may have been a primary emotion that was effecting Patricia and addressing it in the above psychodrama was helpful, but not complete. When a barometer (dysfunctional angry reactions) is persistent after treatment, there may exist *another primary emotion* that needs to be addressed. Patricia's mother told Patricia and her grief therapist that Patricia's father died of cancer. Patricia's father actually died of AIDs and her mother chose to edit reality and tell Patricia that her father died of cancer, making AIDS a secret. Patricia learned the truth when a visiting six-year-old cousin suddenly blurted out to Patricia, "I hear your father died of AIDS." Patricia's mother did not know that Patricia had learned the truth and a "wedge" had been placed between them. The wedge was not Patricia's cousin because her cousin was only stating the truth. The wedge was a *lie* that Patricia's mother chose to use and when the truth was revealed, other primary emotions developed within Patricia. Patricia did not know what AIDS was, but the fact that it was a secret created the primary emotions of embarrassment and humiliation within her. Having this information, the grief therapist could continue therapy by utilizing the same structure. Patricia created concrete symbols (she drew projective pictures) of her primary emotions of embarrassment and humiliation. Patricia was allowed to express anger toward these symbols as she did the previous symbol of abandonment. As her anger dissipated, she was counseled with more psychodrama. With action-focused techniques Patricia and her mother rehearsed the adaptive behavioral option of openly talking about dad, his death, and AIDS. Patricia's barometer of displacing anger finally subsided.

When this structure for managing children's dysfunctional angry reactions is utilized and destructive anger persists, it is helpful for the grief therapist to determine if another primary emotion may need to be addressed.

PARENT SUGGESTION

Children will find out the truth. If parents do not offer the truth or edit the truth, a wedge comes between parents and children when children eventually learn the truth. Often it is painful to tell children the truth, but it is destructive to the healing process when reality is edited. When reality is edited there is a greater opportunity for children to develop destructive magical thought and cognitive distortions. Children do not need gory details about a death, but they do need to know the truth.

SUMMARY OF A PLAN OF TREATMENT
FOR ANGER MANAGEMENT

Barometers

Children utilizing anger in a dysfunctional manner usually have barometers, which are often identified as destructive angry behavioral reactions. Often their angry behavioral reactions have magical thought attached. Barometers act as a device for measuring the existence of children's primary emotions as well as the effectiveness of treatment.

Targets

A well-defined target offers children the opposite of displacement. Angry children who are well established with their attachment to the Model of Magical Thought tend to displace anger in many directions. When children displace anger, they do not focus on their actual loss(es) and the normal grief emotions that are causing them emotional pain. Children expressing anger toward a target representing the original loss and/or a symbol representing primary emotions related to the original loss reduces displacement. A target can be utilized to direct children back to the tasks of healthy mourning as experiencing and expressing primary emotions is consistent with Task II—to work through the pain of grief.

Primitive Plan of Treatment

"What have you done to make yourself feel better or help yourself with this loss?" is a question that reflects Task III (how are you going to adjust to your environment?). Angry children usually create plans to help themselves, but their incomplete cognition often results in primitive plans that are not always functional and at times quite destructive. Often the functional parts of children's primitive plans can be utilized, but their primitive plans require additional structure and modification from adults who think abstractly, resulting in a more effective plan of treatment reflecting the tasks of healthy mourning.

Identifying the Primary Emotions

The ability to conclude that primary emotions exist and are often demonstrated via anger requires abstract reasoning. Children who think concretely and those with developing abstraction are often very immature in their abstract abilities. When children create plans to help themselves, they often exclude their primary emotions, which are abstract. A grief therapist can assess if children's primary emotions are included in children's primitive plans of treatment. When primary emotions are not in place, grief therapists can help incorporate children's primary emotions by helping children identify primary emotions and by developing plans of treatment that actively incorporate children's primary emotions.

Express Anger at the Symbol of Primary Emotion

Children can be redirected to express anger at a symbol of the primary emotion. This therapeutic redirection of anger expressed toward the symbol of the primary emotion will usually allow children's anger to dissipate instead of generate. Once children's anger dissipates, the primary emotion is usually easily accessed.

Treatment of the Primary Emotions

There are several goals when grief therapists are treating bereaved children's primary emotions and offering more complete interpretations to children's loss experiences.

Goal 1

Often connected to children's primary emotions are their incomplete or inaccurate interpretations of their loss experience. One of the goals of treatment is to offer children a more comprehensive and accurate understanding of their loss experience, by correcting their distorted interpretations that may promote magical thought and enhance dysfunctional anger reactions.

Goal 2

Another goal of treatment is to help children adjust to their loss by developing and rehearsing more adaptive behavioral responses to reduce anger and advocate for the tasks of healthy mourning. Children can rehearse behavior that reflects the tasks of healthy mourning.

Goal 3

Another goal of treatment is to help children stop the expression of dysfunctional angry reactions and allow them to experience and express all of the normal emotions of mourning.

CHAPTER 7

A Special Note for Parents

Parents are the most special people in children's lives. Children naturally look to their parents as mentors to assist them in understanding the experiences of their lives, including losses such as the death of a loved one. This is an ominous task for parents as grief is an overwhelming experience that children do not understand. To complicate further, our society does not easily embrace the natural process of death and grief. As the many facets of this culture have come together in what is termed a "melting pot," the unique rituals that our ancestors utilized to effectively manage the process of mourning have vanished. Death and grief are thinly discussed topics, which create considerable and sometimes traumatic impact on children and families.

These factors make the job of parenting children who are in a process of mourning quite important. This book discusses the healthy and unhealthy elements of mourning, defining unhealthy mourning as laced with destructive magical thought. By understanding the principles in this book and using it as a reference, parents will have an enhanced ability to recognize unhealthy grief reactions in children. This book offers parents with bereaved children the following skills:

- Parents can more easily recognize children's destructive magical thought related to children's process of mourning.
- Parents have a greater understanding of the goals that grief therapists are attempting to attain when offering grief therapy to children.
- Parents understand the normality and purposes of children's healthy grief emotions.
- Parents understand that children have two cognitive fields (concrete and abstract), which offer children different interpretations of death and grief. Parents also have two techniques to assess children's abstract reasoning.

153

Here is a list of more ideas that may be of value to parents who have bereaved children:

1. Parents can take children for an interview/assessment by a qualified grief therapist every several months for a mental health check up. The Model of Magical Thought demonstrated how bereaved children ingrained in destructive magical thought have the potential to eventually develop either strong defense mechanisms or personality disorders. A qualified grief therapist can review a bereaved child's progress to determine if there has been any development of destructive magical thought creating a complicated process of mourning. It is important to locate a therapist who specializes in childhood development and in the treatment of grief, as using therapeutic techniques that a therapist would use for other mental health issues, such as depression, may be inappropriate and, at times, dangerous. Associations, funeral homes, and local hospices often are the best resources for attaining referrals of qualified grief therapists who understand childhood development and grief therapy. Consider the following suggestions in determining if a therapist is a qualified grief therapist:

- Ask the therapist what professional associations he or she maintains membership which reflects grief and bereavement. Hopefully grief therapists belong to associations such as the American Academy of Bereavement, the Hospice Foundation, the National Center for Death Education, King's College Centre for Education about Death and Bereavement, and other grief and bereavement organizations that offer continued education in this specialized area. Most national organizations have regional membership and regional associations, which can offer excellent referral sources.

- One of the most pivotal questions to ask therapists to determine if they are knowledgeable grief therapists is this, "Whose tasks of mourning do you use in your grief therapy?" If a therapist mentions Alan Wolfelt, William Worden, Therese Rando, or others who are known for developing the tasks of mourning, there is a greater probability that the therapist is a grief therapist. Tasks of mourning are the guideposts to healthy grief. If a therapist is not aware that there are defined tasks of mourning, then the therapist may treat grief as depression is treated, which can be quite dangerous. For example, children need to embrace grief with all normal grief emotions being experienced and expressed. Depression is to be eliminated either through medication or prescribed activities that counter depression. Therapists unaware of the tasks of mourning may make suggestions that grief reactions should be medicated or offer activities that distract from the process of mourning. Both of these methods could be counter to the tasks of healthy mourning. Grief therapists should also have thorough knowledge of the various types of complicated mourning, such as the typology of complicated mourning described in Dr. Therese Rando's book (1993), "The Treatment of Complicated Mourning."

- The longest established local hospices are usually the best facilities to attain a referral for an excellent grief therapist. Physicians tend to refer to psychiatrists and very few psychiatrists have been trained in grief and bereavement. Hospice staffs, who are actively engaged in assisting bereaved families, usually have a full awareness of the various services and grief therapists available in their community.

- Licensing boards for various professional groups are helpful as they can offer information on which professionals have met the minimum requirements to receive a license. Licensing boards can also give public information about which therapists have had a significant number of complaints.

- Most mental health professionals who specialize in grief and bereavement have more training beyond the minimum requirements needed to maintain their license. For example, I am a Certified School Psychologist and a Licensed Clinical Psychologist in two states, but none of these four licensing boards require that this author take specialized grief and bereavement training to maintain these four licenses. Most mental health professionals who specialize in grief and bereavement have additional training offering advanced certificates. For example, the American Academy of Bereavement has a Bereavement Facilitator Certificate that requires four days of comprehensive training with a variety of instructors who specialize in grief and bereavement. Those professionals who are certified need to maintain their specialized certificates by attaining continued hours of training every year, which enhances their expertise. It is important for parents to ask therapists if they maintain certificates for specialized training in the treatment of grief and bereavement.

2. Although mental health check-ups are greatly effective in curbing the development of children's complicated mourning, the reality is that many parents often do not follow this suggestion. For parents who do not follow this suggestion it is helpful to know the "red flags" suggesting that initiating therapy is vital. Remember the following "red flags" that suggest that therapy is necessary:

- Persistent magical thought expressed by children may suggest that cognitive distortions are fueling their magical thought, leading to the potential development of defense mechanisms and/or personality disorder.
- Extremes in children's behavior including excessive isolation, dependency reactions, aggressive acts, avoidance, and perfectionism.
- Excessive and continuous emotional reactions, especially those that are not consistent with the normal grief emotions such as embarrassment, humiliation, feeling betrayed, abandonment, phobias, and panic.
- When children never demonstrate the normal grief emotions, there is great concern that children may be developing destructive magical thought.
- A pattern of displacement of children's angers onto others without any expression of the normal grief emotions.
- Children's unwillingness to talk about the dead loved one.
- Children's deep feelings of discouragement, hopelessness, and helplessness.
- Children's loss of interest in any positive interaction with friends and family.
- Suicidal and homicidal ideation and talk.

3. Parents can model the expression of healthy but often painful grief emotions. Children are looking to parents as mentors through the process of mourning, so it is helpful if parents are demonstrating healthy mourning and allowing children to see parents' progress. Caring parents may accept the cultural magical thought that if they do not express their emotions, their children will feel better. The normal grief emotions are helpful as they have purposes that were mentioned in Chapter 1. One purpose that the normal grief emotions share is that people who are mourning can bond together when they experience normal grief emotions. When parents and children do not express and bond with their normal grief emotions, they may stop a healthy process of mourning and create destructive magical thought. Families expressing normal grief emotions bond together and create a safe environment to express their normal grief emotions.

4. Parents can assist children in developing safe spots at home and at school. Parents offering safe spots to bereaved children help develop empowerment by giving children a choice to choose where to have a grief reaction. Consider the following guidelines for developing structured safe spots for bereaved children:

- Children can be told about a safe spot that their parents had when they were children or currently have. It is helpful for parents to recall a favorite place where they would go to feel safe and secure. Parents, teachers, and grief therapists can also give examples of other bereaved children's safe spots that were developed at home and at school. Children need concrete examples of safe spots.
- Children can draw pictures of actual safe spots that they would like to have at school and at home. Parents can tell children that they can put any items in these pictures that they want that helps them feel safe. One suggestion that many children appreciate is to get a shirt of the loved one who died and together a parent and child can stuff this shirt with cotton and sew it. The result is a huggable shirt the child can hold and hug when in a safe spot.
- Safe spots from the children's drawings can be actually created and implemented. Typically it is not difficult for families to duplicate a safe spot at home. The school safe spot may require creative modification. One of the favorite places children pick as a safe spot at school is the nurse's office. This may be a practical locale for some schools and not for others. In some schools, the school nurse is not available every day. In other schools, the school nurse may be too far away from the child's classroom. Several creative modifications have been developed by teachers who have made cardboard rooms in the classroom as safe spots, converted a portion of coatrooms into safe spots, created safe circles in the classroom, and created safe spots within the school secretary's office. One very important requirement is occasional adult monitoring of children when children are in their safe spots.
- Children can be taught to give adults visual cues (tug on their ear, hand signals) to signal parents and teachers that they are going to their safe spots. A visual signal offers the assisting adults knowledge that children need to go to a safe spot and also helps the adults keep a frequency count of children's grief reactions.
- A ten-to-fifteen minute time-period is usually suggested for children to spend in their safe spot. Younger children can be taught to set a timer.
- Children can be instructed to do a variety of activities while they are in their safe spots. Children may have intense emotional reactions, feel a need to hug the stuffed shirt, write in a journal, draw pictures that express their grief emotions, etc. It is usually best if children's time spent in a safe spot is unstructured and children are allowed the freedom to do what they want—assuming that they are not being destructive. Once they have

completed what they need to do in their safe spot, they can go back to the classroom.

- Parents and teachers can keep frequency counts tabulated reflecting the number of times per day a child uses a safe spot. The frequency count, based on children's visits to a safe spot, offers extremely valuable information to assisting adults. As an example, after Joey's father died a safe spot at school was designed for him. He usually averaged four to five visits to his safe spot per day while attending school. Every Monday he would go to his safe spot twenty to twenty-five times during the school day. Having Joey's frequency counts helped the school psychologist realize that Joey was struggling every Monday. The school psychologist assumed that the weekends may be difficult for Joey and his family. However, when the school psychologist asked Joey about Joey's increased reactions on Monday, Joey revealed a magical thought. Joey responded to the school psychologist's questions about Monday by saying, "My dad died on Monday and my cousin died on Monday. So if anyone in my family is going to die it will be on a Monday." When adults help children develop safe spots and track frequency counts, children can reveal grief reactions that may go unnoticed without safe spots. Children who are not expressing emotional reactions about the death of a loved one will often utilize a safe spot when it is offered, which has helped many children eventually express their normal grief emotions.

- If children become manipulative with their safe spots, further structure can be offered to children. Occasionally teachers may have a child who goes to a safe spot thirty to forty times per day. The teacher is getting feedback that the child is waving to his or her friends on the way to the safe spot and not utilizing the safe spot appropriately. Mentioned earlier in this book was the realization that children have grief reactions five to seven times per day. It is a good assumption that most children will average three to five grief reactions per day at school. Children who are manipulative with their safe spot may actually need their safe spot at times, so taking their safe spots away is not a good option. To help reduce this manipulative quality within some children, the attending adults may have to structure children's safe spots. Children could be instructed that they can have one safe spot time in the morning, one in the afternoon, and two floater times they can use whenever they need. This additional structure allows manipulative children to have safe spots without unlimited access.

- When parents take children on vacation, items can be taken from each safe spot and a safe spot can be duplicated in the car during travel and at the vacation site. This is very helpful to families that go to the same resort or cabin every year, but are now going to the same vacation site without their dead loved one. If children go to the traditional family vacation site, they will often attempt to re-create what they had before their loved one died. Their attempts to re-create are valuable as they reveal the reality of the death, which reduces children's unhealthy denial. If children are allowed to develop safe spots at the traditional family vacation site, frequency counts can continue and children will feel the empowerment of a safe spot when they are experiencing "attempts to re-create."
- Finally, the utilization of safe spots offers barometers. When children are allowed to have safe spots indefinitely, children may eventually use their safe spot less frequently or not at all. When this lessened need for a safe spot naturally occurs, children may be demonstrating that the they are progressing through a process of healthy mourning.

Developing safe spots is one of the easiest techniques for adults to incorporate for children and safe spots have many benefits. Safe spots offer children empowerment as children have a choice of where they will express grief emotions. Safe spots allow adults to monitor and gather information from children. For example, parents' and teachers' utilization of frequency counts reflect the number of times children use safe spots per day, which may signal increased grief reactions allowing caregivers the opportunity to investigate.

5. Children tend to think in concrete terms. Even adolescents who have abstract reasoning have very immature abstraction and limited experience in exercising abstraction, which allows them to easily revert back to concrete thought processes. Children need abstract thinking adults to offer children structure and more options for the healing of their grief. Children who think concretely may develop only one solution for a difficult grief issue. Parents can offer many options that children may not be able to generate due to their concrete cognition. One important service parents can offer their children is to give children a broader variety of suggestions on how to handle difficult grief situations and then behaviorally rehearse, so children can see the suggestions in concrete form. This technique offers children additional tools for handling the many difficult issues that grief offers them.

6. Parents can help children understand the funeral process by explaining to children the process involved in a visitation and funeral

or by taking children to the funeral of someone with whom they were not emotionally involved, such as a family friend or distant relative. The visitation and funeral are filled with abstract rituals that children may not understand. Children simply need to be offered knowledge of the ritual of the visitation and the funeral. For instance, one common issue with children regarding funerals is the ritual of walking up to the casket and seeing the dead loved one for the last time. Many children do not realize that it is the last time they will ever see their dead loved one, which creates a variety of emotional states that may interfere with their process of mourning. A simple explanation to children that this is the last viewing of their dead loved one could eliminate considerable complications.

Another common issue is "clean up." Children within the early development of abstract thought define funerals and funeral homes as frightening. If children have a structured tour and are allowed to open doors at the funeral home and feel the freedom to ask questions about the funeral process and the funeral home, they will "clean up" frightening distorted thoughts with truth and reality about the funeral home.

7. At the funeral home, parents can ask funeral directors for what this author terms the "precious hour." The "precious hour" is an hour of time at the funeral homes that is an option for each family member to attend. The "precious hour" involves giving permission to family members (including children) to have an hour of time to personalize the funeral process. During the "precious hour" family members can take pictures of the deceased, caress the deceased, ask any questions about the funeral process, have explanations of the rituals at the funeral home, create rituals, and generally design the funeral so it is meaningful and personalized. The "precious hour" can create memories that are lasting and quite healing.

8. The combination of individual therapy and support group is very effective service that assists children who are mourning. Individual therapy for bereaved children does not have to be weekly therapy. The suggestion of a regular "mental health check-up" for children every several months, with the advocacy of several sessions when the grief therapist and parents deem it necessary is usually sufficient for individual therapy (unless there is a very complicated process of mourning). The goal of the grief therapist is to ensure that children are progressing within the tasks of healthy mourning. It is not the goal of the grief therapist to take away the pain of children's normal grief emotions.

Support groups for children are usually offered in two forms. One structure of support groups is to be a continuous group. In a continuous support group, the group is ongoing and children are involved in the group as long as they are in need. A second structure for support groups is time-limited, where there is a definite number of sessions over a period of weeks or months. There are advantages to both types of support groups and grief therapists may be able to assess which is the best structure for particular children. One of the advantages of a continuous support group is that it is always there when it is needed. In a continuous support group, children within the group are at different levels of healing which offers children a concrete representation of the process of healthy mourning. Continuous support groups offer children a light structure, allowing children to freely discuss whatever they need to discuss about their grief. The time-limited support group is usually more structured and offers a curriculum of specific topics for each group. For example, I prefer to have ten sessions, (1 session every other week stretching to 20 weeks of involvement), each session discussing specific grief topics such as "attempts to re-create," anguish, adaptive behavior, etc. It is also helpful to have parent support groups in conjunction with children's support groups, so everyone is learning and progressing together.

Neither structure of support groups is better as each has its advantages and disadvantages. Children differ and a qualified grief therapist would be able to determine which type of support group is best for each individual child.

9. This culture places considerable pressure on parents to keep their children happy. Parents have a strong internal desire to do everything they can to develop happy children. Developing happy children is an admirable goal, but not a realistic goal when children are mourning. Watching children experience anguish is not pleasant, and many parents with a caring and protective heart, who do not understand the process of mourning, may try to stop their children's anguish by attempting to keep children happy. Distracting with "happy" activities is a great cure for depression, but it can be destructive to the process of mourning. Parents can offer children protection by advocating that their children be allowed to experience and express all normal grief emotions. The only exception is that children should not be allowed to become continually aggressive and destructive in their behavioral reactions. All of the normal grief emotions have specific purposes. As described earlier, the emotion of anguish is directly connected to love. When parents attempt to eliminate their children's expression of anguish, parents may not realize that they are attempting to stop children from expressing love. When parents with good intentions stop children's "attempt to re-create," parents may not realize that they are enhancing children's denial of the reality of the

death of a loved one. Parents can protect their children by ensuring that their children are allowed to feel, experience, and bond with others as they experience and express all the normal grief emotions.

10. Parents can advocate that their children always be offered an understanding of truth and reality regarding loss experiences. A grief therapist became very upset with me at one of my seminars when she asked how I would tell a five-year-old child that the child's grandfather took a gun and shot himself in the head. I answered, "I would tell the child that the grandfather took a gun and shot himself in the head." The grief therapist was very concerned that this comment may spawn suicidal tendencies within this child. There is wisdom behind the notion that when someone important to a child models suicide, the chances the child may suicide will increase. If a parent decides to withhold telling this child that the grandfather committed suicide, might the child hear from other sources that the grandfather committed suicide? It is very probable that the child will overhear a conversation about the suicide or get the information from a relative. When a child learns that the child's parents did not tell the truth, a wedge may enter their relationship. When this wedge of truth occurs, many potentially destructive elements may unfold. Consider several possible results to withholding the truth from children:

A. Children may conclude that their parents do not think they could adequately handle the truth. This may be a belief that children accept evolving with and attaching to the development of their personality, especially if parents have a habit of withholding truth about important issues.

B. As children become teenagers other distressing emotional experiences usually occur. Teenagers may choose to not tell their parents about these issues because teenagers may model their parents' withholding of the truth.

C. If parents ignore discussing a loved one's suicide, the result may enhance fertile ground for the development of magical thought. Children may develop heroic fantasies about the bravery a loved one demonstrated by committing suicide. These fantasies may result in children glorifying the dead loved one and suicide. The glorification of suicide may increase the risk of children eventually committing suicide.

Painful reality can be processed and healed if truth is the foundation for healing. Editing truth, keeping secrets, and distorting reality results in a greater opportunity for children to develop destructive magical thought. Truth and reality offer people the opportunity to bond and for parents to express to their children that they can handle the realities of life together. Obviously, parents would not want to offer all of the graphic and gory details of a loved one's suicide. Parents need to offer children the essential truth and more. In the above case the essential truth is that the grandfather took a gun and shot himself in the head. The "more" is continued talks about the reactions of the survivors and discussion about coping and not choosing to commit suicide. Children will model the coping mechanisms of parents. If parents withhold and edit truth, children will often model and develop the same dysfunctional reactions. Parents and children can manage reality, but there is no effective way to manage distortions and half-truths.

SUMMARY

Parents are the most important people in children's lives and there is no replacement for quality and caring parents. Quality and caring parents, coupled with knowledge about grief, are the best assets for assisting children who are mourning the death of a loved one. The goal is not to be perfect parents raising perfect children. The goal for parents is to allow children to express the tasks of healthy mourning in many creative avenues. It is helpful if parents utilize the tasks of healthy mourning, have a sensitive ear to children's magical thought, understand that complicated mourning could have lifelong effects, and be prepared to help children rehearse behavior that reflects the tasks of healthy mourning.

CHAPTER 8

Magical Thoughts of Adults and Our Society

Many of our ancestors knew how to process healthy mourning much better than current society in the United States. Although there have been considerable advantages to being a melting pot, one of the disadvantages is the loss of valuable grief rituals and views on death by the many ethnic groups of this nation. For many cultures, death is a natural part of life that is actively engaged through a pattern of rituals that reflect healthy mourning. The current routine and ritual-lacking funeral process that exists in the United States has created insulation from the reality of death. The greater the insulation this culture offers its members from the reality of death, the greater risk children of this culture have in developing destructive magical thought. Consider how the funeral process of today has insulated people from their dead loved ones, as well as the reality of death which enables greater potential for the development of children's destructive magical thought:

- Make-up is placed on the dead loved one's face, fostering magical thought that the dead should not look dead. America is one of the few societies that attempts to make its dead look alive.

- Funeral directors routinely close the doors at the funeral home so families do not view or participate in the closing of the casket. Families viewing and participating in the closing of the casket was and is a valuable ritual for families and friends to perform together that reinforces the reality of the death.

- By not having the funeral at home, there are time limits on how long families can be engaged with their dead loved ones. This restriction reduces many activities and rituals families can perform together in the presence of their dead loved ones.

- The food is gone. Often many ethnic groups, who have the funeral in their home, serve food. The family's sharing of food at the funeral, a shared ritual with friends, has disappeared. The ritual of eating now occurs at a "hall," without the comfort of the home climate and familiar surroundings, often creating an awkward feeling.

• Families no longer watch the casket being lowered into the grave-site, offering further insulation from the reality of death. This is a ritual that, when it does occur, families recall and appreciate.

• Few families perform the valuable ritual of throwing dirt on top of the caskets of their dead loved ones.

• Families do not view the bodies of their dead loved ones at the gravesite. One of the concerns, of our society and funeral directors, is to avoid having families view the bodies of their dead loved ones at the gravesite. Many people have great concern that the seal of the casket not be disturbed to insure that the dead body continues to be preserved. Preserving a dead body seems to have many magical overtones in American society. Why does America value preserving a dead body? It is understandable that the body needs to be preserved long enough for a visitation and funeral, but why is it important that the casket be sealed and never open again to preserve the body? What is magical about preserving a dead body from the natural processes of decay? Decay is a part of the natural process of life and death. Why not let it happen? This culture's resistance to breaking a casket seal is one of the main reasons the casket is not opened at the gravesite. Another reason is that funeral directors are responding to the wants of their clients and clients want the seal secured. The priority of this seal, designed to inhibit the natural process of decay that occurs after death, has stopped the wonderful and important ritual of families viewing the body one last time at the gravesite. Nature has designed dead bodies to decay. What magical thought exists in this culture that suggests that preserving a dead body is necessary? Eternity, sur-viving beyond death, narcissism, legacy, etc.? It may be very help-ful and consistent with the tasks of mourning for families to see the body of the dead loved one at the gravesite.

• When funeral homes cremate a dead body the cremation occurs in isolation and families in American society never witness the burn-ing of their dead loved one. If the reader is from the United States, you may be cringing with this last point regarding cremation. Why would anyone want to see the burning body of a dead loved one? If children witnessed this burning, would it not create for children a post-traumatic stress disorder (PTSD)? In the culture of India, when a loved one dies, the entire community (the youngest child to the oldest adult) gathers wood and places it within the center of their community. The body of the dead loved one is placed on top of the wood for everyone to witness. The body is burned as onlookers watch. Then family and friends gather the ashes and go home. The children involved in this ritual do not experience PTSD. Concrete thinking children attending this ritual have the benefit of experiencing this entire funeral activity which offers concrete reality, leaving little room for the development of destructive magical thought. In the United States, the last time a child sees his or her mother, mother is alive. Then the child is told that mother is dead and has been placed in an urn. This child does not have the complete concrete experience, allowing ample room for the development of destructive magical thought. Why? Because our society promotes rules that suggest people within this culture cannot and should not look at death. In fact, many people in American society cannot look at the leading cause of death—aging.

As I was watching the local news in a city where I was presenting a seminar, I witnessed a news item that was broadcast on all three local network affiliates. The news item was about a home for the elderly. Three months previously, a wrinkle cream company had fifteen elderly people put wrinkle cream on the right side of their faces and this continued for three months. For this news story, all fifteen elderly people were shoulder-to-shoulder, in a line in front of the news cameras. They were asked to turn right and when they did, fifteen younger looking faces appeared. They were then all asked to turn left, and there were fifteen older and wrinkled faces. This is one example of our society stating that the natural process of aging is not good, not attractive, and not valued. American society suggests that everyone wants to live a long life, but no one wants to get old. Watching this one news item and many other media messages have convinced me that American society has difficulty not only confronting death and grief, but also with the natural and normal process of aging which eventually leads to death.

THE FUNCTIONS OF MAGICAL THOUGHT OF THIS SOCIETY

There is magical thought advocated by our society that has an array of functions that inhibit healthy mourning:

Insulation

One of the functions of American society's magical thought is to insulate its members from death and from actively engaging within the process of mourning. Often non-bereaved people give people who are mourning advice to take their grief elsewhere, reducing the concept of community grief and insulating the non-bereaved from the bereaved. For example:

- Although support groups are helpful and productive, they offer non-bereaved people an easy option contrary to the original intent of support groups. Instead of offering the productive benefits of community mourning, some non-bereaved people view support groups as the place where bereaved people should go to mourn, separating non-bereaved from the bereaved. Using support groups to offer separation also promotes the idea that bereaved people should mourn only with other bereaved people. Similar to the concept that those with polio should be isolated so it does not spread. This attitude of separation suggests that bereaved people should collectively isolate to mourn. It further suggests that the non-bereaved should not have to be involved or included in the process of mourning and have nothing to offer those who are mourning.

- American society also suggests that family members should be the first priority to assisting people who are mourning. This notion fails in the face that many extended families are separated by distance. Society further suggests that those who do not have extended family available should go to support groups. If the support group is not helping, the suggestion of going to a therapist is often offered. These three suggestions are sound advice but they also demonstrate the layers of insulation between the bereaved and non-bereaved.

Quick Fix

Another function of society's magical thought is to offer quick fixes to those who are mourning, which results in a lack of support for progression with the tasks of healthy mourning. Here are several common examples:

- "Put it out of your mind."
  This quick fix is a societal response that advocates denial. It advocates that people magically eliminate the death and their normal grief emotions from their mind, which results in eliminating healthy mourning. This suggestion is counter to all the purposes to normal grief emotions as well as all of the tasks of healthy mourning.

- "If you let your grief out, your grief will be gone."
  This quick fix offers the bereaved the magical thought that there is an actual end point to the process of mourning, which does not exist in reality. This quick fix suggests that only expressing the emotional responses of grief will cure the bereaved. This quick fix ignores the tasks of adjusting to the environment where the dead loved one is missing, investing in other relationships, and a complete recall of the entire memory of the dead loved one. This quick fix offers the magical thought that only expressing emotions will cure grief and offer an end point to the process of mourning.

- "Just believe in God and you will feel fine."
  OUCH! While believing in God is beautiful advice, the notion that believing in God will eliminate the pain of grief is magical and destructive. A belief in God, religion, and spirituality can greatly advance progress with the tasks of mourning and offer families and communities a greater level of communication with grief issues. When considering the purposes of the normal grief emotions, there are important lessons to be learned when people are in the process of mourning. If a society, community, or church convinces its people that believing in God can stop the normal grief emotions, important lessons are not learned. Often these healthy lessons are lost and replaced by judgments about one's level of faith being inadequate. Even those who have a very strong faith should feel their normal grief emotions.

- "Why don't you move?"
  Many people in American society offer this quick fix suggestion, which greatly inhibits people's progress with the healthy tasks of mourning; especially adjusting to the environment where the deceased is missing as well as remembering the complete and accurate memory of the dead loved one. It is difficult for a bereaved person to adjust to an environment when the bereaved person has moved from the environment. The environment where the dead loved one lived also brings forth considerable memory of the dead loved one.

- "Get it behind you."
  How? Usually the answer is one or a combination of the four suggestions listed above.

Many of these quick fixes reflect "McDonald's Magical Thought" in American society that suggests there are quick solutions or easy one-step methods to fixing problems, including grief.

Eliminate Emotions

Another function of American society's magical thought is that the emotional expression of grief needs to be contained or eliminated. Consider these magical cures of grief:

- "It's God's will" suggests that those who are mourning should not hurt because this was God's idea and since it was God's idea, it is not a problem.
- "All I have to do is to go through the stages of grief and I will complete my mourning" supports a fantasy of a step-by-step manual for the process of mourning with a well-defined end. But grief never goes completely away. The treatment goals for the bereaved include the healthy and manageable process of mourning, not the elimination of mourning.
- "Time heals all wounds" suggests to those who are mourning that all they have to do is wait and grief will leave. This expression also suggests that the non-bereaved do not have a function with helping the bereaved, as only time can heal the wounds of grief.
- "Quit feeling sorry for yourself" suggests that the normal grief emotions are interpreted as pity for self. This statement effectively squelches the normal grief emotions, including their valuable purposes.
- "Silence is strength" is a common 1950's cultural magical thought for males that stops expression of the normal grief emotions. The expression of mourning is quite important and training a segment of society to not express emotions is dangerous. Another version is "Big boys don't cry." Males in this society who have never shed a tear have had significant losses. Who trained them to be that way? Mothers and fathers have promoted this belief that it is not masculine to cry and this still occurs today. The inverse of this expression is the potentially dangerous magical thought, "Big boys take action."
- "Protect children from grief by not taking them to the visitation and funeral" suggests the magical thought that avoidance will assist children to not feel the normal grief emotions. This suggestion actually takes the concrete experience of the visitation and the funeral away from concrete thinking children, increasing the potential for the development of destructive magical thought.

- "Don't feel bad, you have other children (or siblings)." This magical thought suggests that grief is not justified because the bereaved person has other people in their family. This is a skewed and unhealthy version of looking at the brighter side of life.
- "Everything happens for the best." OUCH! Who decided that everything happens for the best? Was the Oklahoma City bombing an event that happened for the best? Was the Paduka school slayings an event that happened for the best? Was a sniper's nest outside of a school designed to kill students an event that happened for the best? Of course not! It would be "best" if all of those people were still alive, but reality dictates that they are not alive. The "second best" is for the survivors of all those tragic losses to mourn in a healthy manner, but it would be "best" if their loved ones were back.
- "They deserved it!" "She knew smoking would kill her and she kept right on smoking" or "He kept eating all that fast food even after the doctor warned him" or "It's his own fault for taking illegal drugs and contracting AIDS." The message of these statements suggests that since loved ones were responsible for their demise, survivors should not hurt.
- The pop songs of our society that tend to scoff at emotional expression such as "Don't Worry, Be Happy" or "Get Over It" are problematic. The message of this music is that emotions should be easy to eliminate with a subtle and sometimes blatant statement that if a person cannot "get over it," something is wrong with that person.
- Parental protection of children is a priority in this country, which benefits the survival of children. Parental protection can complicate grief when a loved one has died and parents start to protect (eliminate) children from the visitation, funeral, and mourning process. One common parental myth is that if children see the dead loved one at the visitation/funeral, the viewing of this reality will be harmful to children. Experience with children who are mourning suggests the opposite. When children attend the visitation and funeral, it allows them to have the concrete experience, which is a wonderful advantage that may stifle the development of destructive magical thought. If children do not have this concrete experience, there is fertile ground for the development of destructive magical thought. Parental protection of children is admirable, but parent protection by eliminating reality and truth has harmful effects for children and their relationships with parents.

THE TRICKLE DOWN EFFECT

I once told a colleague who had experienced considerable grief as a child that society's and parental ability or lack of ability to adapt to loss has a trickle down effect on children. He responded, "Trickle down? It's a downpour!"

We live in a society that does not express grief well and it eventually affects children as they are developing. The lack of good communication about grief in this society offers many gaps that children may fill with destructive magical thought. The good news is that our society is getting better.

- There has been more quality research in the last five to ten years on the issue of grief than ever before. Grief is becoming well defined with typology of complicated mourning.
- In the last twenty years the hospice movement has raised awareness about death, grief, and death education. The original and long-standing hospices have been leaders in effective care for the terminally ill, allowing clients to die with dignity and at home.
- The death education movement is progressing as research about the effects of death education is starting to surface in the research literature.
- The Internet offers thousands of resources related to grief, bereavement, hospice, and the funeral industry.
- Quality books for children of various ages, professionals, caregivers, and volunteers to those who are dying, as well as to those who are mourning, have increased.

The taboo of death is lessening, but it is still deeply rooted in American society. Within the last twenty years there has been a movement from many academies, institutes, foundations, and universities in the direction of gaining knowledge about death and grief with the goal of dispersing that knowledge. The one death that would be a blessing, is the death of this taboo.

CHAPTER 9

Final Thoughts

The tasks of healthy mourning are the guideposts for advocating a healthy and productive process of mourning. When children become ingrained in a system of complicated mourning saturated with magical thought, they usually develop dysfunctional behavioral reactions. Children need guidance by adults who can assist children back to the tasks of healthy mourning. The important adults in children's lives can utilize the Model of Magical Thought to determine the existence of complicated mourning. Parents and grief therapists can utilize the Model of Magical Thought to identify the clinical point of treatment for bereaved children that they are assisting. Therapeutic strategies, such as those designed with action-focused techniques, can be utilized to eliminate children's magical thought and to help children rehearse and incorporate behavior that is functional and in accordance with the tasks of healthy mourning.

When the process of mourning is healthy, the learning experiences children receive from loss and grief are founded on truth and reality, which can enhance children's lives for a lifetime. Let me tell you one story of my own:

I was sixteen years old when my ninety-year-old Irish grandmother died. I recall attending her visitation packed with people, as she had eight boys that lived in the same small town. Everyone knew her and her family. I was sitting in a hallway of the funeral home with my sixteen-year-old cousin when we noticed a strange sight entering the funeral home. Typically everyone who attended an Irish wake back in the 1960s was well dressed. The strange sight was a very large man who was dirty and dressed in dusty overalls with an old bent hat. I recall thinking that he looked out-of-place. This large old man filled a loveseat in the hallway across the room where my grandmother was lying in her casket. He did not go into the main visitation room. As he sat in the hallway and gazed at her, huge tears fell from his face. My family was buzzing because no one knew who he was and why he would be crying about my grandmother's death. Finally, my mother went to him and asked him who he was and how he knew Mrs. Fogarty. He told this story with delayed and immature English:

> I sell vegetables. Every summer I go from house to house to sell my vegetables. Most people don't even open the door to me. When I go to Mrs. Fogarty's house, she let me come in. She have me sit at her kitchen table and talks with me. She looks at my vegetables and buys all of them. While she is talking to me, she takes out her pots and pans. She starts cooking. She feeds me. She feeds me a feast and we talk for hours. Then she gives me leftovers and some extra money to take to my family. She treated me like a king.

I heard him tell this story when I was sixteen years old, but it fell on dead ears. It offered no impact, I thought. I was wrong. The experience of my grandmother and this old man who sold vegetables cataloged into the back on my mind and fermented for years. It waited to come out at the right moment and it did.

Much later in my life, this old man's story about my grandmother helped me to realize that life is an incredible privilege and an opportunity to have an impact on people, which is essential, powerful, wonderful, and spiritual. This seemingly helpless and very frail ninety-year-old woman was anything but helpless, as she created a deep and influential impact on everyone around her. There are countless stories of her impact on others and when she is spoken of thirty years after her death, a smile travels across the faces of those who knew her.

One of my goals in life has been to offer a similar impact on the lives of others. I hope this book has offered a positive impact to you as well as the children you are assisting.

APPENDIX A

Resources for Action-Focused Techniques

- American Society of Group Therapy and Psychodrama
  301 N. Harrison St., Suite 508
  Princeton, NJ 08540
  Phone: (609) 452-1339
  E-mail: edgarcia@artswire.org

- National Coalition of Arts Therapies Association (NCATA)
  2000 Century Plaza, Suite 108
  Columbia, MD 21044
  Phone: (410) 997-4040

- National Association of Drama Therapy
  15245 Shady Grove Rd., Suite 130
  Rockville, MD 20850
  Phone: (301) 258-9210

The next listing offers the most thorough recommended readings on the topics of action-focused therapy, psychodrama, sculpting, and drama-therapy available. This listing is on the Internet and offers over 100 references of books and articles:

- Homepage: Psychodrama Links
  Internet Address:
      http:/home.erols.com//leopold/Psychodrama.htm

The next listing is one of the best professional journals devoted to action techniques:

- The International Journal of Action Methods
  1319 18th St. NW
  Washington, DC 20036
  Phone: (800) 365-9753

References

American Psychiatric Association (1994), *Diagnostic and Statistical Manual of Mental Disorders—Fourth Edition,* Washington, D.C., pp. 184-186.

Bowlby, John (1979) *The Making and Breaking of Affectional Bonds,* Tavistock Publications, London.

Bowlby, John (1988) *A Secure Base: Parent-Child Attachment and Healthy Human Development,* BasicBooks-Routledge, London.

Britchnell, J. (December 1972) Early Parent Death and Psychiatric Diagnosis, *Social Psychiatry,* 7:4, pp. 202-210.

Burns, David (1999) *The Feeling Good Handbook,* Plume, New York.

Doka, Kenneth (1989) *Disenfranchised Grief: Recognizing Hidden Sorrow,* Lexington Books, Washington, D.C.

Frayn, Douglas (February 1996) Normal and Pathological Variants: Comment, *American Journal of Psychiatry, 153*:2, p. 297.

Freud, Sigmund (1960) Letter to Binswanger (Letter 239). In E. L. Freud (Ed.), *Letters of Sigmund Freud* (Vol. 19). London: Hogarth. (Original work published 1923).

Gorkin, Michael (July 1984) Narcissistic Personality Disorder and Pathological Mourning, *Journal of Contemporary Psychoanalysis, 20*:3, pp. 400-420.

Kübler-Ross, Elisabeth (1969) *On Death and Dying,* The Macmillan Company, London.

Kübler-Ross, Elisabeth (1983) *On Children and Death,* Macmillan Publishing Company, New York.

Lies, Nils (1992) Follow-Ups of Children with ADHD: Review of the Literature, *Acta Psychiatrica Scandanavica, 85*(368, Suppl), 40 pp.

Mallouch, S., Abbey, S., and Gillies, L. (May 1995) The Role of Loss in Treatment Outcomes of Persistent Somatization, *General Hospital Psychiatry, 17*:3, pp. 187-191.

Mazlow, Abraham (1987) *Motivation and Personality—Third Edition,* Harper-Collins, New York.

Mesquite, De Paul and Gilliam, Walter (Spring 1994) Differential Diagnosis of Childhood Depression: Using Morbidity and Symptom Overlap to Generate Multiple Hypothesis, *Child Psychiatry and Human Development, 24*:3, pp. 157-172.

Moreno, J. L. (1964) *Psychodrama, First Volume—Third Edition,* Beacon House, Inc., New York.

Moreno, J. L. (1975) *Psychodrama, Second Volume,* Beacon House, Inc., New York.

Moreno, J. L. (1969) *Psychodrama, Third Volume,* Beacon House Inc., New York.

Parkes, C. M. and Weiss, R. S. (1983) *Recovery from Bereavement,* Basic, New York.

Piaget Jean (1975) *The Origins of Intellect: Piaget's Theory—Second Edition,* W. H. Freeman and Company, San Francisco.

Piaget, Jean (1979) *The Child's Conception of the World,* Littlefield, Adams & Company, New Jersey.

Rando, Therese (1993) *Treatment of Complicated Mourning,* Research Press, Champaign, Illinois, pp. 154-183.

Thomas, Jean (Winter 1995) Traumatic Stress Disorder Presents as Hyperactivity and Disruptive Behavior, *Infant Mental Health Journal, 16*:4, pp. 306-317.

Weller, E., Weller, R., and Fristad, F. (June 1995) Bipolar Disorder in Children: Misdiagnosis, Underdiagnosis, and Future Directions, *Journal of American Academy of Child and Adolescent Psychiatry, 34*:6, pp. 709-714.

Wolfelt, Alan (1988) *Death and Grief: A Guide for Clergy,* Accelerated Development, Indiana.

Wolfelt, Alan (March/April 1991) Toward an Understanding of Complicated Grief, *The American Journal of Hospice & Palliative Care, VI, 8*:2, pp. 28-30.

Worden, W. J. (1982) *Grief Counseling & Grief Therapy,* Springer, New York.

Worden, W. J. (1991) *Grief Counseling & Grief Therapy—Second Edition,* Springer, New York.

Index

Abandonment, 141, 148
Absent grief, 71–72
Absent mourning, 75
Absorbing the surrounding
  emotions/tensions, 28
Abstract reasoning
  academic technique used to access
    presence of, 39, 40
  adolescence abstract thought
    unleashed, 44–45
  changes the playing field, 41–44
  cleaning up distortions about death,
    42–43
  concrete thinking to, transition from,
    26–27
  emotions have a greater impact on
    children with, 41
  frightening, death and things
    associated with death are,
    42–43
  interactive technique used to access
    presence of, 39–40
  process which has a beginning and
    an end, 41
  religious and spiritual beliefs, 45–46
Academic technique used to access
    presence of abstract reasoning,
    39, 40
Accept the reality of the loss, 65–66
  bedroom of a dead family member,
    preserved, 81, 83
  dialogues with dead family
    members, 89, 90
  re-create situations/experiences,
    attempts to, 94–96
  waiting for a dead family member to
    return home, 67–68
Action-focused techniques
  advantages of using, 103–105
  defining, 103

[Action-focused techniques]
  empowerment, regaining feelings of,
    30–34
  examples of, 112–120
  interview process, 108–110
  parental involvement, 104, 110–111,
    120–128
  psychodrama, 128–134
  purposes of, five, 105–108
  resources for, 175
  sharing magical thought and
    sculpting, the family, 120–128
  summary, 134–135
Adaptive behavioral responses,
    rehearsing, 106–107, 109
Adjust to the environment in which
    the deceased is missing, 66
  bedroom of a dead family member,
    preserved, 82, 84
  dialogues with dead family
    members, 89, 91
  fear of having an emotional reaction,
    69
  re-create situations/experiences,
    attempts to, 95
Adolescence abstract thought
    unleashed, 44–45
Aging, societal views on, 167
AIDS, 148
Anger
  barometers, 139
  converted grief, 73
  drawing, 141–144
  empathy used to push parental
    buttons, 47
  express anger toward the symbol of
    the primary emotion, 143–144,
    148, 150
  at females, 138–147
  healthy and unhealthy, 137–138

[Anger]
normal grief emotions and their purposes, 17–19, 21
personality disorders, 59–61
primary emotions, 137, 140–142
primitive plan of treatment, 140
secondary emotions, 138
summary of a plan of treatment for, 149–151
symbolize the primary emotion in concrete form, 143
targets for, 139–140, 149
treatment of primary emotions, 144–147
Anguish, 15–17, 21, 61–62, 68, 73
Assessment/interview by a qualified grief therapist, 154–155
Attachment problems, 27–29
Attention deficit hyperactivity disorder (ADHD), 9–12, 29

Bad or good concept, 35
Barometers, 139, 148, 149, 159
Basic skills category of cognition, 25, 27
Bedroom of a dead family member, preserved, 81–88
Behavioral rehearsal to promote emotional bonding, 131–132, 134
Best, everything happens for the best, 171
Betrayal, 141
Bonding, 27–28, 131–132, 134
Bowlby, John, 27
Burns, David, 53
Button pushing, 18–20, 47

Captain James T. Kirk Syndrome, 44–45
Cardboard figures, making, 88
Child custody disputes, 112–120
Chronic grief, 74
Chronic mourning, 78
Cleaning up distortions about death, 42–43, 160
Cognition, children's
absorbing the surrounding emotions/tensions, 28
abstract reasoning category of, 26–27, 39–47
action-focused techniques, 31–34
attachment problems, 27–29
basic skills category of, 25, 27
concrete thinking category of, 26–27, 29–30, 34–39
distortions, cognitive, 53–61

[Cognition, children's]
empowerment, regaining feelings of, 30–34
imitation, 29
incomplete, 6
memory, 29–30
summary, chapter, 47–48
variable among children of the same age, 26
Commotion, 9–13, 21, 29
Comparisons of people alive vs. dead, promoting, 93
Complicated mourning
absent grief, 71–72
chronic grief, 74
converted grief, 73
distorted grief, 72–73
"R" response, Rando's six, 74–78
Concrete thinking
abstract reasoning, transition into, 26–27
empowerment, regaining feelings of, 30–34
finality of death, 35–36
good or bad concept, 35
grief, exercise for helping children understand, 36–39
here-and-now, living in the, 34–35
memory, 29–30
mini-movies in your head, 30
misinterpretation, susceptible to, 36
power attributed to parents, 36
Conflicted mourning, 76–77
Conversion from unhealthy model of magical thought to tasks of healthy mourning
bedroom of a dead family member, preserved, 86–88
defining conversion, 85–86
dialogues with dead family members, 92–94
re-create situations/experiences, attempts to, 98–99
Converted grief, 73
Convert relationship with deceased from one of presence to a relationship of memory, 66
bedroom of a dead family member, preserved, 83, 85
dialogues with dead family members, 90, 91
editing reality, 70–71
re-create situations/experiences, attempts to, 95–96
Cremation, 166–167

Culturally-based magical thought, 79–80

Defense mechanism, 54, 55–61, 73
Delayed mourning, 75
Demonstrating the dysfunctional dynamics of grief-related situations, 105, 109
Denial and children's attempts to re-create situations/ experiences, 14–15
Dependency, 55–56
Depression, 142
Diagnostic and Statistical Manual of Mental Disorders, 9
Dialogues with dead family members, 88–94
Disappointment, 141
Disenfranchised grief, 78–80
Displacement, 73
Distorted grief, 72–73
Distorted mourning, 76
Distortions, cognitive, 53–61
Divorce, grief due to, 50–51, 73
Doka, Kenneth, 1, 71, 79
Drawing, 92, 141–144, 157

Egocentricity of children, 35–36
Embarrassment, 142, 148
Emotions
    absorbing the surrounding emotions/tensions, 28
    abstract reasoning, 41
    elimination of, 170–171
    fear of having an emotional reaction, 69
    mimicking emotional bonding, 27
    parents, children wanting emotional reactions from their, 128–132
    primary, 42–47, 137, 148, 150
    purpose of, 6
    rehearsal to promote emotional bonding, 131–132, 134
    secondary, 138
    See also Normal grief emotions and their purposes; *individual subject headings*
Empathy, 47
Empowerment, regaining feelings of, 30–34
Everything happens for the best, 171
Expert in the eyes of children, how to be an, 5–6

Express anger toward the symbol of the primary emotion, 143–144, 148, 150

Families expressing grief emotions together, 156
    See also Parents
Feeling Good Handbook, The (Burns), 53
Feeling posters, 87
Females, anger directed at, 138–147
Finality of death, 35–36
Food and the funeral process, 165–166
Freud, Sigmund, 15
Frightening, death and things associated with death are, 42–43, 160
Funeral process, 42–43, 159–160, 165–167
Future, jumping to conclusions about the, 55

Gifts offered to and by children, 3–4
God's will, 170
Good or bad concept, 35
Graveside therapy, 92
Grief Counseling & Grief Therapy (Worden), 66
Grief emotions, 6, 36–39
    See also Normal grief emotions and their purposes; *individual subject headings*
Guilt, 20–22

Happy activities, distracting with, 161–162
Healthy mourning distorted by destructive magical thought
    accept the reality of the loss, 67–68
    adjust to the environment in which the deceased is missing, 69
    complicated mourning, 71–74
    convert relationship with deceased from one of presence to a relationship of memory, 70–71
    dialogues with dead family members, 88–90
    disenfranchised grief, 78–80
    Model of Magical Thought with the tasks of mourning, utilizing, 80–85
    re-create situations/experiences, attempts to, 94–96
    "R" response, Rando's six, 74–78
    summary, chapter, 99–100, 173–174
    tying it all together, 71

[Healthy mourning distorted by destructive magical thought]
withdraw emotional energy and reinvest it in another relationship, 69–70
Worden's five tasks of health mourning, 65–66
work through to the pain of grief, 68
See also Conversion from unhealthy model of magical thought to tasks of healthy mourning; Normal grief emotions and their purposes
Helplessness, 142
Here-and-now, living in the, 34–35
Hopelessness, 142
Humiliation, 148
Hyperactivity, 10

Imitation, 29
Impulsivity, 10
Inattention, 10
Individual therapy and action-focused techniques, 105
Infant's need for sameness, 27
Inhibited mourning, 76
Insulation, 168
Interactive technique used to access presence of abstract reasoning, 39–40
Interview/assessment by a qualified grief therapist, 154–155
Interview process, action-focused, 108–110
Intrusiveness of adults, 31–34, 108, 109–110
Invincibility, feelings of, 44–45

Jumping to conclusions about the future, 55

Kübler-Ross, Elisabeth, 1

Licensing boards for various professional groups, 155
Lifeline, child's, 94

Magical thoughts advocated by society inhibiting healthy mourning
aging, societal views on, 167
eliminate emotions, 170–171
funeral process, 165–167
insulation, 168
quick fixes, 168–170
trickle down effect, 172

[Magical thoughts advocated by society inhibiting healthy mourning]
See also Conversion from unhealthy model of magical thought to tasks of healthy mourning; Model of Magical Thought; individual subject headings
Make-up placed on the dead, 165
Marketing to children, 111
Meaningful conversation, children seeking, 132–134
Media influencing children with frightening concepts of death, 43
Memory
establishing a relationship with the memory of the dead loved one, 66–67, 97
infancy, 27
intrusiveness of adults, 21
preschool and early elementary school years, 29–30
See also Convert relationship with deceased from one of presence to a relationship of memory
Mimicking emotional bonding, 27
Mini-movies in your head, 30
Model of Magical Thought
cognitive distortions, 53–54
defense mechanism, 54
defining magical thought, 49–51, 53
mourning, tasks of, 80–99
personality development and the process of mourning, 52–54
personality disorder, 54–62
power-based catalysts of magical thought, 51–52
questions leading to the development of, 1–2
secondary gains, examples of the power of, 62–63
summary, chapter, 63, 100–101
See also Conversion from unhealthy model of magical thought to tasks of healthy mourning; Magical thoughts advocated by society inhibiting healthy mourning; individual subject headings
Moreno, J. L., 128

Name replacement, 98
Normalcy and action-focused techniques, 110

Normal grief emotions and their
  purposes
  anger, 17–19, 21
  anguish, 15–17
  commotion, 9–13
  defining normal grief emotions, 6
  families expressing grief emotions
    together, 156
  guilt, 20–22
  numb and stunned reaction, 6–9
  passive-aggressive reactions, 18–20
  re-create situations/experiences,
    attempts to, 13–15
  summary, chapter, 21–23
  See also Healthy mourning distorted
    by destructive magical thought
Numb and stunned reaction, 6–9,
  21

Parents
  action-focused techniques and family
    involvement, 104, 110–111,
    120–128
  assessment/interview by a qualified
    grief therapist, 154–155
  emotional reactions of, children
    wanting to see, 128–132
  happy activities, distracting with,
    161–162
  options for healing grief offered by,
    159
  power attributed to, 36
  precious hour and funeral process,
    160
  qualifications of a grief therapist,
    154–155
  red flags that suggest that therapy
    is necessary, 155–156
  safe spot, making a, 156–159
  sharing magical thought and
    sculpture, the family,
    120–128
  special note to, 155–163
  summary, chapter, 163
  support groups for children, 160–161
  truth, telling the, 162–163
Parents, advice/suggestions for
  abstract reasoning, 41, 42, 44
  action-focused techniques, 111,
    135
  anguish, 17
  attachment problems, 28–29
  attention deficit hyperactivity
    disorder, 12
  issues that need solutions, offering,
    34

[Parents, advice/suggestions for]
  Model of Magical Thought, 63, 101
  normal grief emotions and their
    purposes, 22
  numb and stunned reaction, 6–9
  passive-aggressive reactions, 20
  primary emotions, 142
  reality of death, rituals and the, 36
  re-create situations/experiences,
    attempts to, 15
  religious beliefs, 45
  truth, telling the, 149
Passive-aggressive reactions, 18–20,
  22, 47
Past wounds and psychodrama,
  132–134
People replace, 69–70
Perfectionism, 58–59
Personality development and the
  process of mourning, 52–54
Personality disorder, 54–62
Pet replacement, 79
Photographs, 99, 104
  See also Sculpture
Physical deterioration, 44
Piaget, Jean, 1, 25–26, 50
Pop songs, 171
Posters, feeling, 87
Post-traumatic stress disorder
  (PTSD), 11
Power attributed to parents, 36
Power-based catalysts of magical
  thought, 51–52, 55–61, 73
Precious hour and funeral process, 160
Preserved bedroom of a dead family
  member, 81–88
Primary emotions, 137, 140–147, 150
Primitive plan of treatment, 140,
  149–150
Probe for magical thoughts, 109,
  123–124
Projective device, action-focused
  techniques used as a, 107,
  109
Protecting children from grief, 170, 171
Psychodrama, 128–134, 144–147

Qualifications of a grief therapist,
  154–155
Quick fixes for those who are
  mourning, 168–170

Rando, Therese, 1, 13–14, 65, 71,
  74–78
Realistic concerns, plan solutions for,
  117, 124–125

Re-create situations/experiences, attempts to, 13–15, 21, 72–73, 94–99

Red flags that suggest that therapy is necessary, 3, 155–156

Rehearsal to promote emotional bonding, behavioral, 131–132, 134

Rehearsing adaptive behavioral responses, 106–107, 109

Religious and spiritual beliefs, 36, 45–46

Revenge, 47

Role replacement, 98

Role switching, 117–119, 125–126

"R" response, Rando's six, 74–78

Sadness, 142

Safe spot, making a, 69, 87, 92–93, 156–159

Sameness, infant's need for, 27

Sculpture
  child custody disputes, 112–120
  sharing magical thoughts, the family, 120–128

Secondary emotions, 138

Secondary gains, examples of the power of, 62–63

Silence is strength, 170

Six "R" response, Rando's, 74–78

Small talk, children attempting to engage parents in something deeper than, 132–134

Sorry for yourself, quit feeling, 170

Spiritual and religious beliefs, 36, 45–46

Substitution and action-focused techniques, 104

Support groups for children, 160–161

Switching roles, 117–119, 125–126

Symbols of resolution, 108, 109, 119–120, 126–128

Talking as an important part of grief therapy, 111

Target for anger, 139–140, 149

Theorists and their insights/knowledge about grief, 1

3-D picture. See Sculpture

Time heals all wounds, 170

Timing and action-focused techniques, 104, 111

Traumatic stress disorder, 11

Treatment of Complicated Mourning, The (Rando), 155

Trickle down effect, 172

Truth, telling the, 148, 149, 162–163

Unanticipated mourning, 77

Vacations and safe spots, 159

Videotaping, 104

Viewing the bodies of dead loved ones, 165, 166

Visual cues and safe spots, 157

Withdraw emotional energy and reinvest it in another relationship, 66
  bedroom of a dead family member, preserved, 82, 84–85
  dialogues with dead family members, 89–91
  people replace, 69–70
  re-create situations/experiences, attempts to, 95, 96–97

Wolfelt, Alan, 65, 67, 71

Women, anger directed at, 138–147

Worden, William, 1, 65–67

Work through to the pain of grief, 66
  bedroom of a dead family member, preserved, 81–82
  dialogues with dead family members, 89, 90
  inhibiting the expression of grief emotions, 68
  re-create situations/experiences, attempts to, 95, 96